Introduction

Launched in 1955 and looking like a sci-fi design proposal for a future then undreamed of, the Citroën DS became a symbol of something more than just a car. In its advanced thinking it defined a great French era of technology and even of French social science amid an intellectualism, a political and industrial confidence and an engineering education. France began a new age in the 1950s and the DS helped launch that era.

Somehow the DS was more than the sum of its automotive parts. A car, a Citroën and it seems something more – which endures to this day. None of the accolades heaped upon the DS was hype; it really was the height of engineering and design. Yet, curiously, it never received the advanced engine envisaged to complement its overall design. And underneath its advanced body, there lay hydro-pneumatics, and the use of new materials amid new design.

Alongside the DS in the early 1950s, the French produced the world's first twin-engined and swept-wing jet airliner – one with the engines uniquely mounted at the back of the aircraft. This was the elegant Sud Aviation/Aérospatiale Caravelle, an airliner that wiped the complacent British and the Americans off their arrogant aeronautical perches with the shock of its new technology and its wonderful aerodynamics and style. Caravelle created new design thinking, a new 1950s design language – just like the DS did.

The Caravelle and the DS framed a great era in French history and both would sell in America. Imagine, an American airline using a French jet airliner! It happened even as Boeing was expanding. DS shocked the Americans too, but it was a bit too advanced for the mainstream, accountancy-led thinking of Detroit and its carmakers and their set formulas of design, driving and, above all, costs and profit. Yet front-wheel drive and aerodynamics would be seeded into the American automotive psyche by the DS and the subsequent Citroën SM.

Against this backdrop, we were visited by the alien from the galaxy that was the DS – or as Roland Barthes tagged it, *Déesse* (Goddess), in his *Mythologies* as being something that had fallen from the sky on an unsuspecting public. The derived term *Déesse* became a DS colloquialism but DS was the car's name and badge.

The DS was the new *technologie* – aerodynamic, part-plastic, devoid of suspension springs – via its ride-height-adjustable gas and air suspension system and its pump – and built with the world's first synthetic content and moulded dashboard: it had a new seat construction method, and was unusually built up on a part-frame under chassis with bolt-on unstressed body panels. It contained other innovations too. The DS made contemporary 1950s rivals look like antediluvian-design dinosaurs.

America's answer was flashy colours, pointy fins, bling, acres of chrome, sheets of soft steel and sheer horsepower, all wrapped up in huge cars that in general, defined a motorized society but not advanced engineering thinking.

With the exception of the brilliant and innovative Rover P6 series, Britain's answer was to continue to produce square-rigged austerity-cruisers of cars. Germany stayed boxy and upright with one glorious exception – the NSU Ro80 with its Wankel rotary engine and futuristic premonition of a body that took aerodynamic design to new heights:

Quintessential DS. Note Pallas-trim level sill covers, side rubbing strips and C-pillar finish. The 'intergalactic' style and scaling of the DS is very evident here. (Photo Author)

Ro80 arrived over a decade after the DS and only lost the plot due to the failures of its rotary engine design. The DS would stay in production from 1955 to 1975. Along the way it would morph into many variations, with, from 1967, the faired-in, 'cats-eyes' headlamp and nose treatment.

Today, the DS still astounds and has a tribe of dedicated devotees, some of who are so devoted that they are blind to its only significant fault and, attack those who discuss it. Yet the DS deserves its place as a radical disrupter of engineering design and its role in the development of the motor car. Here in the DS, was wrapped an incredible moment in the history of man's motoring and no one should be in any doubt about the DS and its effect.

Yet despite this history of design set off by Citroën with its Traction Avant model in 1936 and the Deux Chevaux/2CV, in 1955 the DS was a shock to a world that

was still turning out box-shaped, rear-wheel-drive cars with wheezing engines, cart-spring suspension and horsehair-stuffed leather seats that filled interiors which resembled those of an Edwardian-era railway carriage or an hotel lounge.

Even the French were shocked by the DS and, in response, in 1957, Citroën produced a lesser-trimmed DS known as the ID – it had less hydraulic features and was cheaper. To confuse things further the ID became the D Special in later years.

The author grew up with a family DS and has owned and driven the DS/ID and Citroën hydro-pneumatic cars all over the world, in France, Australia and in Africa – where many DSs still reside. So herein, is the DS tale, written in a detailed yet accessible style of DS enthusiasm with just one caveat – the car's structural safety design being the elephant in the room and a point of massive contention in the DS

This DS is unusual for its roof contours – because, although a fixed-head saloon, it has a rare, full-length roll-back, soft-roof conversion carried out in Switzerland in very low numbers.
(Photo Author)

British-registered DS in one of the many shades of blue that Citroën offered for its car. The stance of the car at ride height is evident as it serenely cruises past.
(Photo Author)

The essential DS roof-mounted trumpets or coronets, housing the indicator lamps. Seen here in fully trimmed Pallas-type rear C-pillar and rear windscreen detail of DS design delight. (Photo Author)

world. The DS was not the only car that had such issues, so we need to see this facet of the DS in the context of its time.

Should the DS define Citroën as a marque? Many argue that it should and does and has done so for decades, yet that is a singular view that may detract from the achievements of Citroën's wider design work and its range of other cars. But in terms of design bravery, design inspiration and design purity, is any rival obvious? The DS was not without fault, but its achievement and its effect were, and remain, realized upon a global scale.

As a product design and as a piece of social science within a corporate and a French psyche, the DS was and is unique. It was surely the height of design and marketing and the consequent effect of a product defining a brand rather than a brand defining a product. But maybe after the DS Citroën was defined by both these things – car and brand, at the same time.

For a while, alongside the Caravelle, and then Concorde, the DS framed both a national and a European design language. If only today's standards of build quality could have prevented the tarnishing of the DS; if only it had been built as well as Concorde. Despite the caveat, DS can only be called a magnificent event in automotive history. And it still looks as it morphed from a futuristic film where some form of sci-fi animal has been beamed down to earth.

Old DSs also rest up across Asia and Africa and some are still in daily use.

Today, the DS desire, the total enthusiasm for the car continues, and rightly so. French stylist Gerard Godfroy has recently built a new DS coupé to his own design but based on the DS and somehow channelling Bertoni sculpture:

First the Caravelle, then the DS, and then Concorde – all amid an era of French technology and design. This post-1967 DS with slant-front styling is on its highest hydro-pneumatic ride-height setting. (Photo Citroën)

many fans think it is the ultimate DS incarnation, as does this author.

In this CarCraft title, we study the DS and its design and effect, and also pay tribute to the legions of modellers and models that embrace the DS enthusiasm – which remains a global phenomenon. It is fitting that the French company, Norev, should produce the widest and most detailed series of die-cast DS models; Heller model kits of the DS are also superb.

Above all, we best belt-in, grab the single spoke steering wheel, raise the hydro-pneumatic suspension, rev the rather coarse engine, and proceed through the air in a slipstream of Citroënism.

DS the delight, DS the designer spaceship, takes off at this point. If Citroën design and the DS are not your thing, alight here prior to a launch into orbit.

Origins: Autos to Aerodynes

An earlier era: Citroën C Type 12/24 from 1927 in the period before Citroën embraced a revolutionary design language.
(Photo Author)

The 'double chevron' of Citroën was the brand of legend. The DS was the product that unusually was both defined by the brand and yet which then came to redefine the brand – a very unusual trait in the motor industry. Today the new Citroën 'DS' branding tool as a marketing mechanism has little to do with the 'real' DS car.

The DS was engineered and designed by men steeped in the arts of French cars from the 1920s onwards. The great engineering, architecture and art schools of Paris trained many of the men who created Citroën.

We should not forget that the first Englishman to properly fly a powered aircraft a decent distance did it in a French Voisin aircraft and that Voisin's designer, André Lefebvre, became chief engineer at Citroën in the 1930s. The first aircraft to cross the English Channel was French – a fact often forgotten by the British. The American Wright brothers resided in Paris to promote their new aeroplane – not London, not Berlin, not Turin, nor Vienna.

Paris was, from the 1890s to the late 1930s, the crucible of the aeronautical and the automobile design and engineering world and their respective advancements. Despite the legends of Frederick Lanchester in Britain, Ferdinand Porsche in Germany, and Vincenzo Lancia in Italy, it was the likes of Ettore and Jean Bugatti and the French, and notably, Gabriel Voisin, Pierre Cayla, Jacques Gerin, and above all, André Citroën (1878–1935), who, to use a cliché or two, pushed the boundaries and really did think 'outside the box' – did he even believe in the box? – to launch a new era of design and its language.

Gustave Eiffel (who built an early wind tunnel and his famous tower in Paris), Henri Coanda, Alphonse Pénaud, Emile Lavassor, Leon Levavasseur, Gaston Grummer and others were the innovative freethinkers who were part of the great French engineering design movement of this era.

The world's first production monocoque aircraft design with a smooth skin and attention to drag reduction was a monoplane (not a biplane) designed in Paris by Armand Deperdussin in 1912, but it was ignored as the biplane fashion and its string- and wire-built contraptions ruled the air for two decades: latterly the monoplane was 'discovered' in the 1930s, after years of wasted opportunity.

The French really were way ahead, but often ignored by the closed minds of perceived wisdom – itself a contradiction in terms. The DS would suffer a similar fate in its early years.

André Citroën was fascinated by the works of Jules Verne, so future-vision was in his soul. The 1930s/'40s term for an aerodynamically chamfered car was 'streamliner' and it was also applied to railway locomotives, aircraft, one Chrysler car, and a general design movement. But if a car design was truly ellipsoid, radical and super-streamlined, it became something called an 'aerodyne' and it was from the aerodyne movement that stemmed the DS. Aerodyne thinking predated Art Deco and the 1930s streamliners.

Henry Ford? Never to be ignored, but in the 1920s/'30s, he was a purveyor of iron, tin, leaf-springs and V8 lumps whilst the French were racing ahead – in every sense. Edsel Ford's idea for a Lincoln V12 'Zephyr' rear-engined aerodyne of aircraft-type aerodynamic monocoque construction to a design via the mind of visionary futurist designer John Tjaarda (now better known as John Tjaarda van Starkenborgh) and with input from Eugene Gregoire, was an American attempt at an advanced car and it went not very far at all because the US auto industry only made money by giving the car-buying public the very minimum of what the carmakers thought they could prescribe to that public.

At Citroën, under André Citroën and his team, things were different.

Ettore Buggati, who created the world's most advanced iteration of a racing car in his Type 35, was Italian but somehow became French, and so too was Flaminio Bertoni as the man who shaped the Citroën Traction Avant, and the DS.

Designers like Jaray, Rumpler Ledwinka, Porsche and Komenda were Bohemian exceptions to a great era of French automotive advancement. The American designer of 1930s aerodynamic and biomorphic vehicles, Norman Bel Geddes, also supped at the French design cauldron in Paris in the late 1920s. In this great French era, the seeds of the spirit of Citroën, and of the bravery that was the DS, were laid down.

Despite the rise of the German automakers and the technical research of the wind tunnels of Stuttgart, despite Detroit and wonderful design fantasies from Ford and General Motors, and cars like the Pierce Arrow Silver Arrow or the Auburn Cord, Paris, was and remained the centre of an aeronautical, automotive, and architectural design and engineering

The hero and the mover, the man behind it all, visionary André Citroën. Without him and his team, car design would have been very different. (Photo Citroën)

psychology that affected everything it touched or which encountered it.

In 1947, Saab's radical designer Sixten Sason dreamed up his own Saab 92 – a sort of flying saucer of a car – but only after spending time in Paris immersed in the French design language and its effects.

Throw in Art Deco and other movements, the great French painters of the 1920s and 1930s, the World Exhibition of 1925 in Paris which saw all the world's design thinkers flock to the city, and a scene was set where the likes of the DS and the Caravelle could only have come just over twenty years later from such thinking and education.

But, you might ask, why did Renault and Peugeot not produce the radical new age of the car? The answer was that they did not have André Citroën, his mind or his money and his designers and engineers. Only Panhard and the engineers Charles Deutsch and René Bonnet came close to rivalling Citroën for the advanced art of French 'aero' design and aerodynamic excellence.

André Citroën was a serious thinker and a trained engineer, yet he is often described as a 'gambler' but this is a pejorative term used to frame an inaccuracy. In his cars, and his card games, André took strategic decisions and was far from the luxury-lifestyle celebrity so often caricatured. Yet he was an early celebrity; he spent millions revolutionizing the French car industry through the design of his cars. He copied

Early 1920s British-built Citroën production. DS would latterly be built in England at Slough. (Photo Citroën)

Citroën also produced commercial vehicles, taxis, and its famous 'Kegresse' off-road vehicles which Citroën used on a series of global expeditions to profile its talents.

Henry Ford's mass-production processes after a meeting with the great man in 1912, but he did not copy Henry Ford's cars and his by-then out-of-date design and engineering philosophy.

André Citroën, who had made money in his engineering business prior to 1920, produced 'normal' cars from 1921. Before that, he had been involved with the Mors Car Company and Le Zèbre amid a series of limited-production-run early cars. He had in fact overseen the creation of a Mors car that would influence his later thinking. André made money from producing a range of civil and military engineering items, notably gear cogs and bezels – which formed the symbol of the Citroën car company on its badge ever since – gear-cog chevrons.

As early as 1919, Citroën had announced his first car, one designed by Jules Salomon and soon to include the thinking of Edmond Moyet. By 1921, Citroën's new Levallois factory in Paris was to produce its first car and 12,000 cars were soon turned out.

This first true Citroën was the A Type, also known as the Type A, and it was a basic low-cost little car of 1,327cc but it boasted a rare item – an electric self-starter as well as full-lighting kit. Type A also had proper steel wheels, not wooden or wire spoked like so many other cheap cars of the era.

There followed a series of Type B and further Type C Citroëns across the 1920s, each one innovating new ideas and more space and more style. André Citroën created a dream-team of top engineers and designers. These included lead names such as Guillot, Joufret, Dufresne, Louys, and Broglie, Laubard, Norroy, Sallot and Vavon, who all became key contributors.

The B2 was the first all-steel-bodied Citroën and a stepping stone to the use of the monocoque (chassis-less) body design of the later Traction Avant. Before that came the first big Citroëns – the Types 8–15 and the 'Rosalie' with up to 2,460cc and 54bhp engines and luxury trimmed cabins. Special, streamlined bodies were also experimented with on Rosalie-type chassis.

Having succeeded with his cars, the forward-thinking André Citroën wanted to do something new: a stepping stone to the future was required. On the one hand that might be the 2CV, or was it to be the Traction Avant? Both cars emerged from the crucible of Citroën's advanced 1930s design bureau (Bureau d'Etudes) at the Rue du Théâtre, Paris, in the 1930s.

Traction Avant

Always looking for new features for his cars, André Citroën used a French-designed but American-owned new mechanism for

The 1930s–'50s Traction Avant was Citroën's first step on the road to design and driving revolution, sculpted by Bertoni who went on to hand-craft the incredible DS. (Photo Author)

mounting his car engines to make things smoother via a 'floating' engine-to-chassis mount. He also ordered the research and design of a one-piece, chassis-less monocoque bodyshell and he promoted the new front-wheel-drive mechanism to power the car's driving wheels – previously rear wheel-drive had been the norm, even for Citroën. New suspension design that was more technical than the conventional leaf-springs and use of simple bed-type springs, was to become a Citroën innovation too.

A smoother, more aerodynamic body design had been investigated by French and German car designers and André Lefebvre had explored this theme, along with front-wheel drive, at the Voisin car company via the Voisin *laboratoire* car projects; as Voisin's company faltered, Lefebvre moved to a brief tenure at Renault before meeting André Citroën. He joined him in 1933 and further progressed such innovative engineering ideas for the double chevron.

Lefebvre designed an early in-engine clutch for front-wheel-drive applications, dreamed up a continuously variable transmission and began to have thoughts about a utilitarian 'economy' car and a larger car as a VGD – a *voiture de grande diffusion*. The small car would become the 2CV and the big car would, via the Traction Avant of 1936, develop into the DS of 1955. Only the Second World War delayed Lefebvre's design and engineering activity.

Lefebvre was the kingpin in the development of the advanced design of Citroën. Above all, he was the expert in body design, aerodynamics and forward thinking. Others would deal with the detailing, the engine and drivetrain. But Lefebvre also knew about handling and ride, and was open to new thoughts for such. All that was required was the added ingredients of Bertoni on the one hand and on the other, the strategic thinking of Pierre Boulanger, and the resulting outcomes were the defining DNA of what Citroën became in the second half of the twentieth century.

The precursor of the DS, its precursor was the Traction Avant of 1936. This was the car that started the astounding Citroën process, yet it was also the car that partly drove the Citroën car company to financial disaster and into the arms of French investors such as the Michelin Company. Stress, money worries and illness also saw off André Citroën, the great engineer and marketer: he was dead by 1935, owing his bankers hundreds of millions of francs, just as the Traction Avant and its revolution dawned. Michelin (the French tyre company) stepped in and bought a major holding in Citroën which it retained for decades.

The Traction Avant had cost a fortune to create and André had previously overextended himself with new factories and improved conditions for his workers: The Traction Avant would cost more money to productionalize and rectify its problems at its launch. It was not the world's first front-driven car, nor was it the world's first true monocoque car body design. Yet it was the first *mass-production* car to incorporate these features in a mid-range car available to the many not the moneyed elite.

The Traction Avant also added new ideas for independent wishbone/torsion bar suspension, better steering quality, improved engine mountings, a refined

A smaller-engined and purer iteration of basic Traction Avant design. This 'Light' Traction was Slough-built. (Photo Author)

This is the bigger, developed Traction Avant and in fact is a rare Dublin-built example. Note the chevron-grille design and stunning design language. The Traction had *moteur flottant* engine mounts and a 'swan' badge design was used to signify such. (Photo Author)

Traction Avant on steroids – note bigger boot/trunk box and later trim fittings. Low slung and sleek, despite its free-standing front wings/fenders, the car was highly aerodynamic for its era. (Photo Author)

drivetrain, cabin design and style. The one-piece body was also very rigid and safe in a crash – it did not split open like the old-fashioned coach-built, body-on-frame-cars. The body was styled by hand in three days from a picture in the mind's eye to a hand-carved clay model by the Italian-born but French resident Flaminio Bertoni (not to be confused with the famous Italian car designer Bertone). Styled from thought to hand-wrought clay sculpture in days, the Traction Avant was an act of genius. In this car, Bertoni defined a new car design language that remained timeless beyond fashion or foible for nearly twenty years.

From a base-model 7A with a four-cylinder engine, to a roadster soft-top, to a commercial version, and to ever larger models with longer wheelbases and more powerful engines such as the model 11, then the rarer 15/Six, the Traction Avant was the first star in the French industrial design firmament and was to be manufactured in other countries including Great Britain. Sadly, a V8-engined, upmarket version, the 22CV, failed to enter production.

The last of the Traction Avants built (up to 1957) were the 15H-series and these deployed the new Citroën hydro-pneumatic 'air' suspension at the rear wheels – prior to the DS being suspended by such mechanism at all four wheels.

Beyond Lefebvre, key engineers in the realization to Traction Avant were Jean Daninos, Raoul Cuinet, Maurice Julien, Pierre Franchiset, and road test engineer Roger Prud'homme. The car's new wet-liner overhead-valve engine was designed by Maurice Sainturat.

In all, 759,111 Traction Avants were manufactured – making Citroën world famous as a brand.

In the Traction Avant lay cues for the future – a low-slung body, wind tunnel-developed airflow control with lower aerodynamic drag than its rivals: the Traction Avant's coefficient of drag was around Cd 0.42 at a time when most cars had drag coefficients of above Cd 0.55. The car had superb suspension and ride characteristics and enhanced levels of comfort for the driver and passengers.

The 'face' of the Traction Avant which set a Citroën design hallmark through its use of branding, chevron design and sculpted styling. (Photo Author)

Traction Avant was also offered as a delightful two-door hard-top and the soft-top roadster-type seen here hustling up Prescott hill with its rare Michelin-type wheels churning. (Author Photo)

Bertoni worked to reduce aerodynamic drag by moving the Traction Avant towards a more integrated frontal styling motif with faired-in headlamps. (Photo Citroën)

Above: A rare view of Bertoni's original 2CV styling buck. Note the flatter roof shape over the curved roof which entered production. (Photo Author)

It was a huge success and sold all over the world, yet even by 1939, Lefebvre and Boulanger were thinking of something even more radical, but in the Traction Avant, there lay the genesis of the DS itself.

The intervention of the war slowed progress at Citroën so both the 2CV and large 'VGD' car were stalled. It was not until late 1946 that Citroën was able to restart the design process for the production of a both a small car and a big one.

For Citroën the years 1933–39 proved to be significant steps in the evolution of design knowledge and its transfer into cars – despite the death of André Citroën. His team took the Traction Avant to the 22CV V8-engined proposal that so nearly achieved series production (a handful were reputedly built). They came up with the 2CV which, despite being basic, was a car that stunned the perceptions of normality and perceived wisdom. The design team also began thinking of the next big step, the next iteration of a grand Citroën road-cruiser.

Below: The 2CV set in modern times – still on the road despite being an early 1930s design concept. A poor-man's Bugatti perhaps … (Photo Author)

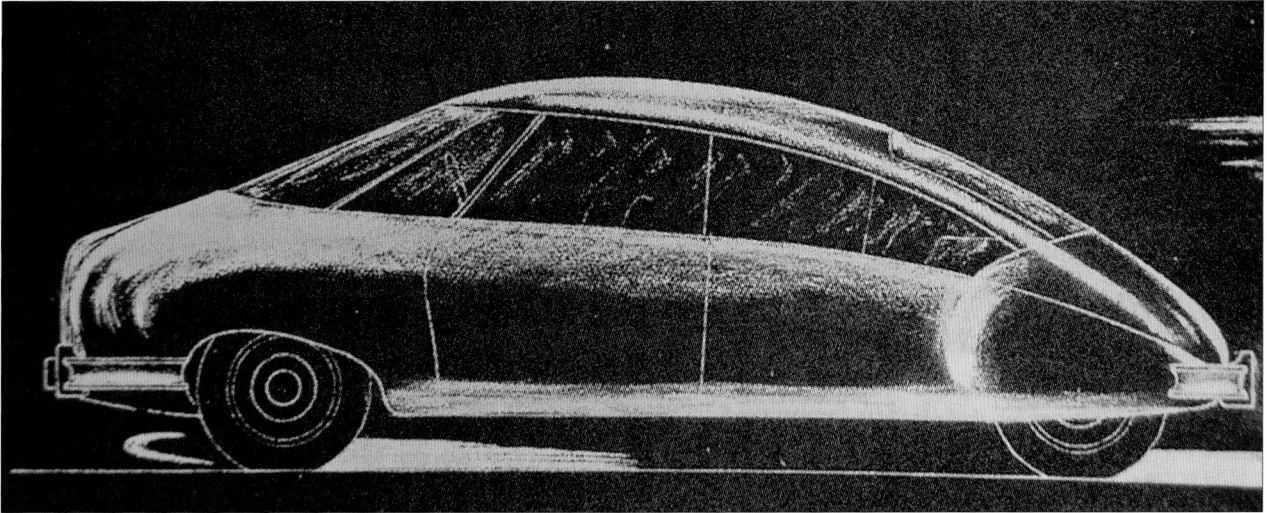

One of Bertoni's famous sketches developing the large Citroën into the DS. The themes of the DS's design language are of course obvious in this biomorphic design. (Photo Citroën)

Designed to be Daring

The idea of a larger, more modern Citroën, one with appeal from mid-range to top of the range, was long thought of. Citroën needed a top-of-the-range model, but it also needed a car with a wider appeal across the French marketplace. Little did it realize that it would create a car that defined its own international marketing niche and model sector.

To achieve this, Citroën would have to be radical. Perhaps Boulanger, Lefebrve and Bertoni were at their best co-operatively, for Lefebrve was always way ahead and now Boulanger had to look at every possible design and engineering possibility to secure yet another advance for Citroën after the Traction Avant – after all, how do you replace a revolution?

Pierre Bercot was Citroën's boss as the DS was created; he was an intellectual who had the vision to see that this new car presented an opportunity to further the status not just of Citroën, but of France and its culture. Alongside the DS's industrial design contemporary that was the advanced Caravelle airliner (and latterly Concorde), it was a chance to frame French technology. So Bercot was key to the plot.

France's roads, even major ones, were in a poor state of repair. After the 1939–45 war, every aspect of France needed rebuilding. Any big new car of appeal needed the suspension and comfort abilities to travel such poor roads. Only Germany had had motorways prior to this period. Lefebvre and Boulanger had already thought about all this, even before the war's further

effect on French infrastructure. And the 2CV's torsion-type suspension design had provided ample experience of the issues.

The Voisin–Lefebvre legacy would again touch Citroën as the idea for a long wheelbase, aerodynamic car became seeded in the thinking for the new car.

DS?

Many experts claim that 'DS' does not, principally, indicate anything whatsoever to do with *Déesse* (Goddess) or any grand intellectual nomenclature as subsequently cited. Instead, DS simply derives from two points: D comes from the basic inherited Traction Avant 11D engine type; S derives from the 'hemi' (hemispherical) design of the cylinder head as expressed in French as *culasse spéciale*. The original '19' in DS 19 indicates the engine's cubic capacity rounded down, e.g. 1,900cc: when that capacity was enlarged, so too was the identifying number – as in DS 20, DS 21 and DS 23. But DS could have stood for Design Special because Bertoni and Citroën created something striking and so futuristic that it was beyond expectation or immediate comprehension.

The halls of the famous motor shows are often filled with advanced styling fantasies that might trickle down in diluted fashion to a car in five or even ten years' time. But what if a carmaker was to present a car so advanced, not just in shape but also in engineering, and that the car was not a 'design special' but a new car – ready for sale?

In 1955, this is what Citroën did as it threw everything at the DS: the impact was massive. At the Paris Motor Show there was a near riot as people jostled to see this incredible new car. Many thousands of orders were taken from the newly affluent French society: over 12,000 orders were taken on the opening day alone, yet Citroën would make less than 100 in the first few months of production. However, in its first full year of production (1956), Citroën managed to produce 98,068 DSs. In the end, the DS sold over 1.3 million examples.

In one day, Citroën had publicly torn up the rules of perceived car-design wisdom, rules burned up in the wake of a car that truly defined the beginning of what we might call Citroën's 'spaceship' years: for it was as if the DS had landed from another planet. It has long been argued just how much the DS touched other carmakers – some say that as no one 'copied' it, its effect was less than claimed, but this is a flawed argument, because the effect of the DS on car design was a long term effect, one that would emerge through various strands of automotive DNA.

The launch of the DS at the 1955 Paris Salon caused a sensation and the car continued to do so right through the 1960s when press and PR were handled by Jean-Paul Cardinal and then Jacques Wolgensinger.

Early studies for a new big Citroën began in 1938. After the Second World War, the DS was soon to be born to the road – in 1955 in its launch form and then in later revised variants across the 1960s and beyond. Here was a car that was not just aerodynamic; it was a completely new design world. Smooth, rounded, plastic-roofed, self-levelling and of utter French style beyond previous classification.

The DS also steered and rode like no other car in the world. The seats were massive armchairs with Dunlopillo cushions and the 'feel' of the philosophy within the car was tangible. The seat covers were manufactured from a new nylon/vinyl-type chemical combination named Rhovyline. Settling into a DS was a previously unexperienced sensation. The car encapsulated the Citroën ethos and has never aged, nor lost its allure. Styled beyond styling and more technically sophisticated than any mass-production car, was this car not the boldest statement of automotive industrial design for the mass car market ever seen?

Led by Aerodynamics

Launched at just under Cd 0.39, by 1967, Citroën's DS was the most aerodynamic production car with a Cd of 0.37 (having been latterly improved by its chiselled front-end restyle of late 1966).

Designer Flaminio Bertoni's intuitive hand had alighted upon the shape of an ellipsoid Goddess yet one rooted in the 'aerodyne' years of the 1920s and 1930s – which Lefebvre had channelled via his sketches for the large new Citroën.

By the mid-1950s, most cars had become square rigged with ungainly cabins or turrets amid a rectangular planform. Some cars would soon even have forward-leaning fronts or noses (as in BMW) and 'stick on' features and swages that interrupted the airflow. Suddenly, aerodynamic drag coefficients for cars began to go up – reversing the previous streamlining trend. This was a bizarre paradox that many major car manufacturers embraced: increasing drag just as knowledge about how to decrease drag was being further expanded.

But for the DS, Citroën stayed with its learning. The animal-like DS was not actually shaped in a wind tunnel but was formed by Bertoni's intuitive hand – a hand that was steeped in the theories of Lefebrve and the forensic analysis techniques of Boulanger. Bertoni shaped his cars himself, but when actually tested in a wind tunnel, the shape was found to be accurate and almost mathematically

Evolving from Traction Avant to DS design. More Bertoni genius seen at sketch stage. (Photo Citroën)

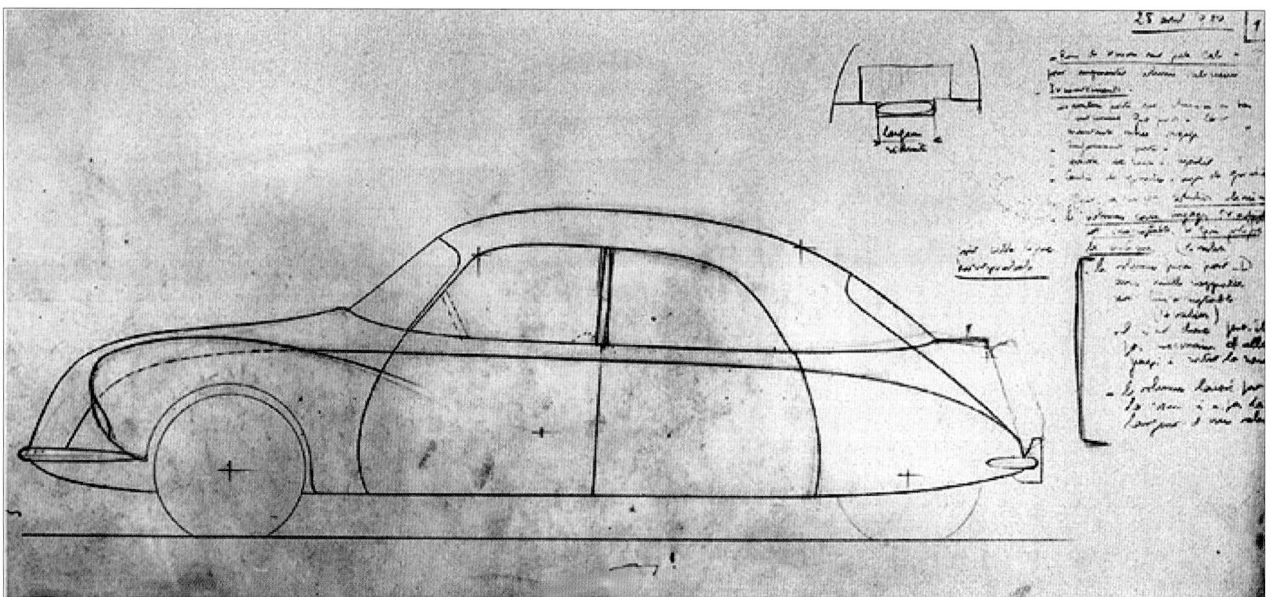

correct when flow was analysed, with only minor alterations being required. Bertoni was inspired by nature and animals and took his design cues from such themes and those of hydrodynamics and aerodynamics. Yet he was apparently a practical thinker and could turn Lefebvre's sketches and thoughts into sculpture.

Bertoni envisaged a tear-dropped monarch of the road, a true French *grande routière* – grand tourer – to tackle long-distance journeys on poorly maintained roads. Via expert input from the DS team, his shape for the DS had numerous highly advanced aerodynamic features and these included a scooped frontal air intake instead of the expected radiator grille and an inbuilt spoiler treatment that altered pressure patterns according to velocity under the front of the car.

There was clear airflow across the front wings/fenders and scuttle region and curved windscreen to reduce turbulence and drag around and along the car, concealed windscreen wipers that lay under a flicked-up trailing edge to the bonnet, and smoothed, sculpted rear panels that narrowed inwards at the rear. There was a defined airflow separation ridge at the top of the rear windscreen.

No other car had ever looked like this. André Lefebvre, André Estaque and Pierre Franchiset were key contributors to the realization of Bertoni's design in the metal. In its blending of two asymmetrical part-elliptical lobes that varied and tapered towards the rear and preserved local airflow velocity and thus delayed airflow separation, the DS used ideas and theories solely then the preserve of a few advanced high-speed supercars and which would take another three decades to become standard practice in the design of mass-market saloon cars.

The visionary Flaminio Bertoni seen with a model of his aerodynamic car design. From this to DS was a short step. (Photo Citroën)

Often forgotten were some last-minute styling revisions forced upon the DS by Citroën's management in response to rumours of rival carmaker's own cigar-shaped or fast-backed four-door coupé design. Bertoni did some top-and-tailing to the DS design, altered the roof and rear window and blended his changes in with the soon-to-be-famous 'Coronet'-type roof lights and fairings mounted on the top of the rear pillars.

Bertoni is associated with the styling of the DS, but others in the body design and fabrication team at Citroën who made the DS were men such as Raymond Ravenel as the project's technical director who did so much to sort out the hydraulic issues – he managed men like André Paget who worked on the DS launch under PR chief Claude Puech – and managed the service recovery programme due to the car's teething problems.

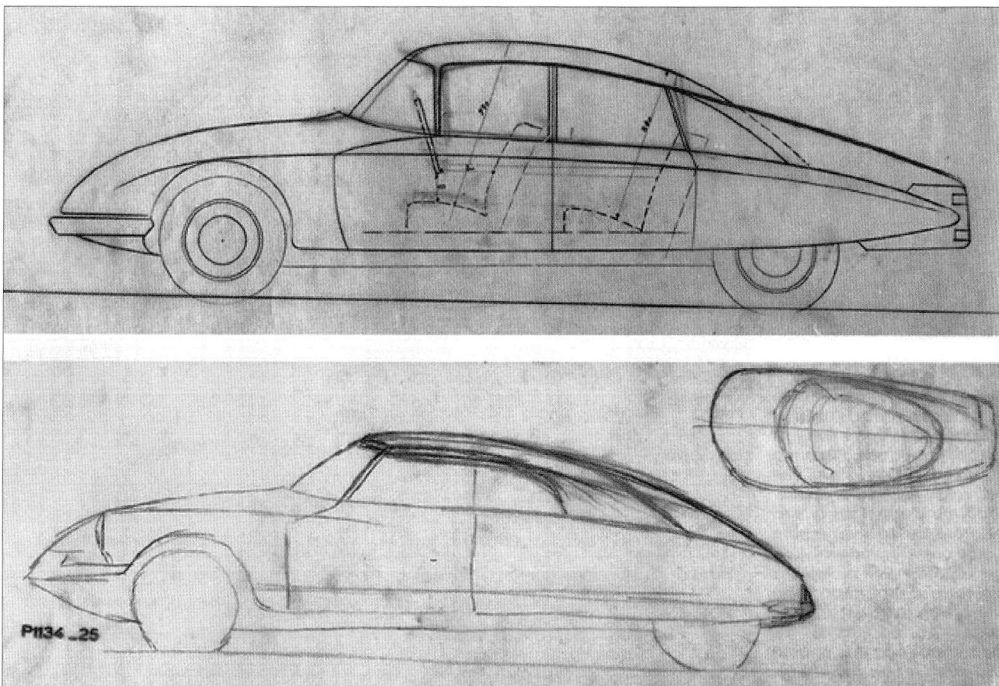

Nearly there – DS design language evolves into a recognizable theme. (Photo Citroën)

In terms of design, men such as Pierre Franchiset and André Estaque were key DS figures. Estaque had joined the company in 1944. He was the design specialist who rose to senior level in the Bureau d'Etudes, the Citroën design study bureau, along with Franchiset, the body engineer who came up with so many of the DS's advanced solutions – from plastics to window design. Franchiset was also the man who engineered the idea of the DS estate and solved many of the DS design issues in his role as a body engineer.

Raoul Henriques Raba worked for the Bureau d'Etudes from 1959 to 1963. Born near Paris in 1930, he was an artist and another sculptor in the team. He had won the Prix de Rome sculpture prize in 1955 – a launching point for a higher profile. He contributed a series of ideas to the development of the DS and, of note, in 1961 did a sketch of a revised headlamp and frontal design motif for the DS that may well have reflected Bertoni's own ideas for such changes – the same ideas that inspired Opron's final 'cats-eyes' treatment for the slant-front DS. The design work of Jean Nicholas is also said to have been part of this 1967 restyle of the DS.

During the later DS years, important roles were also played by Robert Opron as design chief and Michel Harmand, a French car designer with a training in fine art, who was at Citroën from 1964 to 1987. Designer Henri Dargent worked with Bertoni in the vital years from 1957 to 1964: Bertoni may have been the star designer, but Henri Dargent was for many year's Bertoni's assistant at the Bureau d'Etudes. Dargent was a model maker – an expert in plaster and clay. He joined the design office as a junior in 1953, and became Bertoni's assistant in late 1957. It was an association that would prove very fruitful. Like Bertoni, Dargent in the early days had to sculpt in a gypsum-based plaster which was difficult to work and had nowhere near the ease of moulding that self-setting clay and plasticine compounds had in later years. By building large-scale styling models of plaster over a wood and wire skeleton, Bertoni and Dargent sculpted and scaled to judge how light and shaping affected the look of a car from many angles. Here, in these difficult plaster-scraping and sanding techniques, came the clear, open contours of the DS.

How Aerodynamic?
The accuracy of Lefebrve's and Bertoni's work was proven across the decades: here was a car that was aerodynamically stable, kept its windows clean, suffered minimal buffeting and had low lift levels at the rear. Only two issues marred the DS's aerodynamic performance, one was related to the latter 1970s fitting of some very un-Citroën-like 'barn-door' rear-view mirrors on the front doors, and the other

being the effect of a sunroof and radio aerial on airflow separation off the roof, with both factors pushing the Cd figure higher than quoted.

With its domed roof and sharply defined aerodynamic critical separation point ridge at the rear edge of the roof above the rear windscreen, the airflow should have remained attached along the roof to this point and then neatly separated to leave the rear window and boot/trunk in a reducing airflow envelope of wake drag. However, smoke tests in the leading French wind tunnel at Office National d'Etudes et des Recherches Aerospatiales (ONERA) revealed some degree of premature airflow separation upstream of the roof's trailing edge, triggered by the fitting of a sunroof or badly angled roof-mounted aerial.

Although various drag coefficients have been cited and some have suggested the car is not as aerodynamic as claimed, one thing is accepted by automotive experts: Citroën's wind tunnel claims in terms of Cd figures for all its cars have always been legitimate and are unlikely to be exaggerated. In 1955, only the Saab 92 /93 as mass-production cars had a better Cd – that being Cd 0.35. In Britain the 1948 Jowett Javelin, in a blend of pre-war wind tunnel styling from the Lancia era and also perhaps aping the Lincoln Zephyr, the Jowett managed Cd 041.

The early DS/ID shape with upright headlamps sitting atop the front wings was improved upon in airflow terms by the 1967 chamfered nose restyle, but nothing else was changed. However, wider wheels, more chrome trim and the later large area, flat-fronted rear side-view mirrors would not have improved the Cd. Perhaps the DS's only real aerodynamic question mark was its large frontal cross-sectional area which meant that its CdA (or Cx.s) figure was high for its size.

Innovative Engineering
Other new features for the DS were the steering wheel being a revolutionary single spoke. The suspension was – after testing on the Traction Avant 15H – the first use of the oleo or hydro-pneumatic pumped, 'live' pressurized springless system on all four wheels. This was also used to power the high-pressure dual-circuit brakes – along with the steering and, of course, the hydraulically actuated semi-automatic gearbox.

The DS used across its DS and ID variations three differing types of brake actuation mechanisms in its life. Early ID cars had conventional hydraulic brakes, but very quickly the ID range had brakes run from a circuit within the suspension's hydro-pneumatic system as an extra-servo effect, but this proved troublesome and, by late 1961, the ID inherited a version of the DS's full-hydro-pneumatic, pump-driven, button-pedal brakes. Yet this was still not the DS's fully load-limited pressurized

Citroën Coefficient of Drag Figures Cited as Cd for the DS
- Citroën wooden scale model design study test body minus trim and mirrors: Cd 0.326*
- Citroën 1955 production car with standard wheel size and trim: Cd 0.382
- MIRA/Autocar 1982 later post-1967 slant-front car with standard trim: Cd 0.371
- Citroën 1970s D Spécial frontal cross-sectional coefficient: CdA 0.817
- * Scale effects and lack of production trim account for lower Cd figure at ONERA wind tunnel.

André Lefebvre, designer and engineer extraordinaire with roots in the 1920s development of Voisin's cars. From the 1930s onwards he was a defining figure at Citroën and hugely influential for three decades. (Photo Citroën)

A rare view of the DS as a styling model in its original form with small windows in the main rear-pillar. This was the aspect that Bertoni was asked to change for commercial reasons at a very late stage of the DS design. (Photo Citroën)

hydro-pneumatics, but rather a simpler version of it. British-built DS and ID offered their own unique combinations of braking mechanisms, as did the estate car DS.

The 'father' of the Citroën hydro-pneumatic suspension was Paul Mages who had been working on the idea since the late 1930s. His early experiments were a brake-force distribution valve that he wanted to apply to the early commercial vehicles circa 1937. Whether or not he was inspired by the ideas of Cayla, Lefebrve or Gerin dating from the late 1920s is unknown. Mages's main idea was to drive all such supplementary systems that could be hydraulically driven, from an engine-driven pump.

For Mages it was short mental hop to the idea of a suspension, or was it levitating a car using a blend of pressurized air and oil? The oleo-pneumatic as a suspension medium had indeed been hinted at before by the likes of Cayla and Gerin, but here was a cohesive, engineered, fully handed mechanism. By 1938 Mages had built a Traction Avant with hydraulic mechanisms for gears. By 1953 he had done the same thing to a 2CV.

For the DS and subsequent hydro-pneumatically sprung cars, the Citroën system is best briefly explained by stating that a set of pressurized metal spheres containing a mix of gas and fluid are actuated from an engine-driven pump. This system has a 'brain' and is self-monitoring and self-adjusting. The mechanism – the actual working of the act of suspension – is defined by pre-set values and pre-set reactions from the mediums of the suspension itself in an act of hydro-pneumatic interaction.

The springing and damping of the car are created by the action of a fluid upon a gas within individual spheres sited at each wheel, which are themselves controlled by a central pressure regulator and a 'mother' sphere as the core of the system. Because gas will, under compression, harden or become denser – essentially stiffening – but fluid will not, this results in a transmission or transfer of energy to a more malleable element (the gas). Special vents, ports and channels allow the system to be kept 'wet' even when not running.

The DS was the only mass-production car in the world which had its suspension arms mounted on tapered roller bearings, not on cheap synthetic bushes.

From the central control mechanism, a myriad of pipes run off around the car to principally feed the suspension, and then the brakes, steering and gearbox, although some ID models did not have all these other systems powered by the oleo-pneumatic hydraulic unit after it had pressurized the suspension. Certain Slough-built DSs of the 1960s were made with mechanical gearboxes as opposed to being hydraulically actuated.

The main DS suspension pump is fed by a fluid tank which feeds the accumulator or 'heart' of the system. From that point the nitrogen-charged main gas sphere reaches a working pressure that was, at launch, set at 2,490psi and at that pressure effectively 'pumps' the other spheres via the network of piping and then recirculates the central sphere pressure back to the main fluid bath or reservoir.

A drop in pressure below a pre-set level (2,090psi) allows the main pump to re-engage and repressurize the system. The special liquid mineral fluid that powered this system had unique qualities and was initially coloured red, but Citroën changed it to a revised formula that was green.

Famed for its three-position suspension setting, the increased ride-height option allowed DS to traverse snow, mud and minor off-road obstructions. It could, of course, be driven on three wheels and with a flat tyre with no safety compromises – a major safety advance.

Citroën built a new factory at Asnières near Paris to mass-produce the new hydraulic systems for its new car under secrecy and ultra-high-precision component tolerances demanded by the very high-pressure system. In its all-round engineering, DS offered new technology. The details under the skin were fascinating, especially the new suspension design overseen by Paul Mages.

Rolls-Royce and Mercedes Benz later used version of Mages's pump-driven hydro-pneumatics in their cars, as did Austin in its 3.0-litre.

Michelin developed its new 'X' tyre specifically for the DS.

Citroën innovated a new, moulded synthetic material dashboard for the car, another global first because Bertoni created a massive one-piece moulding for the dashboard – a plastics-based piece of space-age sculpture. Of interest, the ellipsoid door armrests were as if one with the car yet were designed not by Bertoni but a Monsieur Michel.

Powerplant

What of the engine to be used? Four or six cylinders – maybe even eight? Bertoni favoured a flat-four or flat-six horizontally opposed engine design to ensure a low line and low centre of gravity. And what of a rotary-cycle engine perhaps? Should a new engine be in-line or vee-angled?

From 1941 there was an ex-Fiat and former Talbot engine designer who had also worked at Citroën, in England. His name was Walter Becchia and, as an Italian, soon forged a friendship with Flaminio Bertoni at the Bureau d'Etudes. By 1943 Becchia was joined at Citroën by his old

Below: An early DS design idea reflecting the 'spaceship' impact of Bertoni's sculpture. (Photo Citroën)

Bottom: From the first idea as sketched, DS frontal design was developed into a sleeker, more rounded form. (Photo Author)

The DS's sub-chassis punt with upper structures built up from it as a skeletal caisson. The floor and sills were very stiff and strong, but contrary to DS enthusiasts' claims of legend, the vertical pillars and roof were not fully integrated into the body which resulted in an issue so sadly long denied. Note the massive engine-support bearer legs. The roof as attached was non-structural and non-load bearing like the doors and wings. (Photo Citroën)

Talbot colleague Lucien Girard who was an expert in fuel air carburation and cylinder head combustion research and brought much Talbot experience with him.

Becchia had been headhunted by Boulanger before the outbreak of the war, not least due to his fame from designing a more efficient 'hemi' head design that improved engine combustion and compression by optimizing the processes within the cylinder head.

A new Citroën engine beckoned, notably a flat-six that expanded upon the 2CV's engine design via Becchia's brilliance: air cooled or water cooled were the options but technical difficulties and post-war budgetary issues actually meant that the DS did not get such a revolutionary air-cooled, flat-six engine to go with its other revolutionary ingredients. Instead, the last Traction Avant's 1,911cc in-line-type engine was repurposed with an alloy crossflow top end and with numerous improvements to its original Maurice Sainturat design. Across the 1960s, the engine was redefined and improved.

The DS used a nylon-moulded cooling fan at a time when other cars used heavy metal for fan blades.

Was this engine less of a failing and more of a compromise?

The fluid used in the DS hydro-pneumatic system was originally the red-coloured, castor-based oil cited as 'LHV'. In 1966 a mineral-based, green-coloured 'LHM' fluid was to be substituted except in North America where legislative issues meant that the American-market cars retained the earlier fluid for some time longer. In fact, North American DSs could also run on a local Lockheed fluid, but use of the wrong fluid could have troublesome results.

Structure

In terms of active safety as driving safety, the DS offered much. Here was a car that could survive a high-speed blowout without skidding or crashing and be driven on three wheels. The DS with its low CG, inboard brakes and brilliant new-technology Michelin X tyres had huge reserves of handling and grip despite its dramatic roll-angles. It understeered, but predictably so. The brakes were powerful, the car's aerodynamic stability superb. Thin pillars – very thin pillars – gave good visibility. The driver was kept comfortable and alert by excellent seating, so long distances could be covered with minimal fatigue even if the rather noisy engine and its block protruded back into the cabin in a manner not originally intended.

The interior was padded and the cabin sealing excellent – noise, vibration and harshness were kept to unprecedented low levels, although the engines were a touch 'rattly'. But there was much that was commendable in terms of design and safety.

Yet DS had an invisible issue.

According to some of the experts, DS's body was very stiff in terms of torsional rigidity and very strong (and by default 'safe'). This was true, but only partly so. Yes, the base unit of the car's sub-chassis was very stiff and strong and expertly engineered, but to suggest that the mid- and upper body and the main, weld-on or bolt-on body pillars and panels were strong, let alone load and impact bearing, is a manipulation, to put it mildly.

Underneath the DS's skin, there lay a skeleton or 'caisson', but unlike that of the human body or an aircraft, it was not integrated to provide impact absorption, load relief, or vertical or lateral compression *throughout* its structure and skin. In effect, the DS was a coach-built composite of 'floating' sections and parts that joined up, allowing easy manufacture and easier-still external body panel replacement.

Having wowed the world with its mass-production monocoque in the Traction

Exquisite DS design captured in the frontal valance of an earlier upright-headlamp car. The chrome strip below the main bumper means the car is a DS not an ID, or does it? Slough-built trim changes can be a devil-in-the-detail affair … (Photo Author)

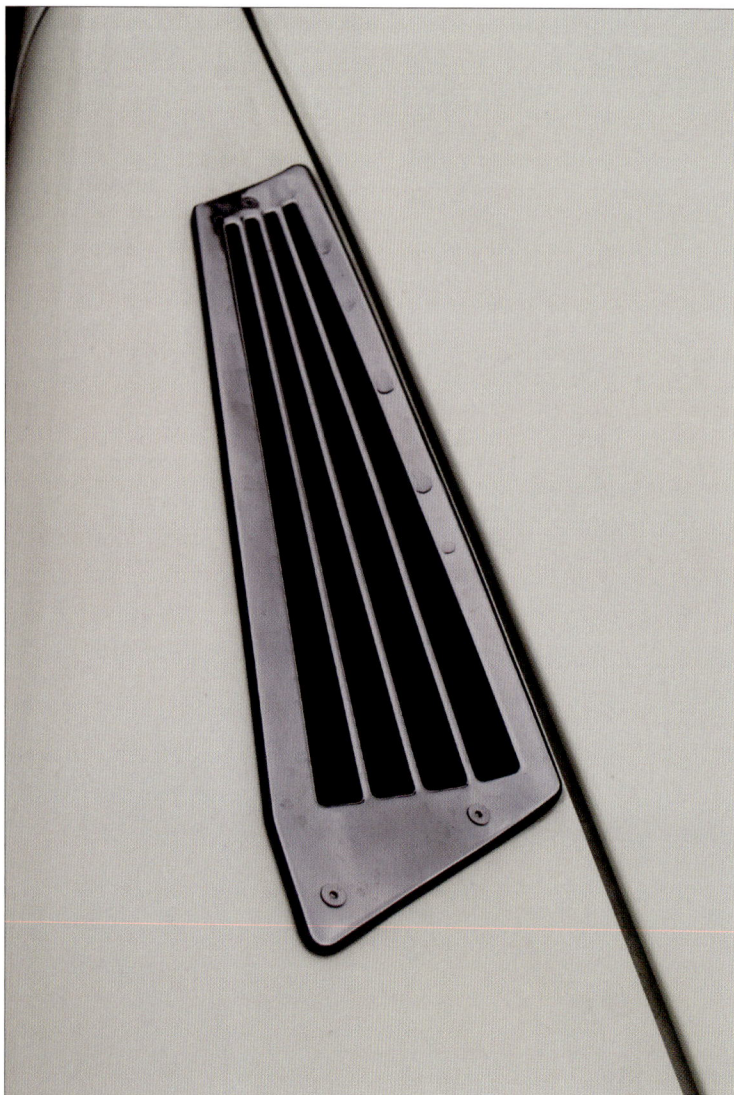

These vents were added to the car's front wings in 1959–62 to aid airflow and cooling in the engine bay. (Photo Author)

Avant, it seems odd that Citroën should abandon such a technique, even more so as the monocoque body was soon to become the standard method for nearly all cars. But abandon the monocoque Citroën did, replacing it for the DS with the floor pan 'punt', a sub-chassis to carry engine and drivetrain loads and a perimeter frame (with massive sills) to provide a base unit upon which completely unstressed, non-loading-bearing body panels and supports could be easily attached (and detached).

Contrary to the claims of certain experts that this technique was new and had not been seen before, such a technique had been seen in a low-volume 1930s Voisin. It was also reflected in the base-chassis origins of the 2CV and the method was quick, cheap and easy to build up for a car body.

Early DS had a glass-fibre resin polyester 'plastic'-moulded non-structural roof panel that could be impregnated with colour (latterly replaced with a metal roof panel). This allowed the roof to be any colour possible. Yet even an early car might be ordered with metal roof if you wanted it finished in natural metal or black hue – because glass fibre could not be sprayed these colours so well.

There were many benefits to the DS's non-monocoque method of body construction: flat steel panels and sections were cheap to manufacture and weld up. The CG was kept low. There is no doubt that the DS's sills and front bulkhead were massive, strong and cleverly designed. It also allowed Citroën to create lighter structures to reduce the DS's overall weight and CG.

So, the DS was also built not as a pure monocoque but as a subframe and sub-chassis that then carried its outer skin as simple unstressed, bolt-on panels. The bonnet was aluminium over a light, steel perimeter frame.

Yet there was to be an issue with the key structural parts of the car's mid and upper cabin. The windscreen (A) pillar and the centre (B) pillar were thin sections of steel simply welded and attached to the underlying frame structure. Of note, the centre B-pillar was not fully integrated into the car's cabin tub structure – it was not integral to the sill or floor pan; this crucial structural pillar was lightly attached top and bottom and effectively 'floated' in its external location and offered very little strength from any angle. Citroën had to add fillets or gussets to the sills-to-B-pillar mountings (into the sills) but even this did not create impact load-path transference.

Like the main windscreen A-pillar design, the centre pillar was attached to a very thin lightweight roof cant rail surround that was devoid of transverse bracing or rollover resistant structure. As late as 1971, Citroën had to revise its attachment and both bolt and weld the roof to this rail to make its attachment stronger (in a heavy crash the original roof would, ultimately, detach from the frame).

The doors of the DS were frameless, the window glass flat, and therefore simple and light. But the doors had no vertical strength to add to the A-, B- and C-pillars: the doors did not form part of the support structure when closed. In 1971, the door design and locking mechanism had to be modified to meet new US legislation. So too did certain engine-bay crossmembers need to be welded and reinforced.

At the rear at the C-pillars and under the rear seat and bulkhead, the DS was strong, but again, this was of little relevance in a heavy frontal crash. So, while the DS was stiff and strong low down in its cabin tub, the vital, impact-absorbing main structures of the car were allegedly thin gauged and in part most non-structural items were 'flocked' to the under structure.

In fact, when converting the DS into a soft-top car, the usual problems of body flex in soft-top car conversion were absent – because removing the roof had little effect – as it was a non-structural item of little original strength to the car. So, the normal body-flex and scuttle-shake caused by roof removal to a monocoque car was absent.

This was proof then that DS had a strong, stiff lower chassis base, so strong that chopping off the roof made no difference! Yet also proof that above the sills and floor line, the vital roof and roof pillars were effectively non-structural and therefore offered minimal strength just where it was most needed in a car at the vital A- and B-pillar and roof section. People who deny the DS's weak upper body argument have difficulty explaining their reasoning around such paradoxical facts.

The outcome of this strong floor punt base unit but non-structural upper body design was that the DS performed poorly in frontal, offset or side impact at even moderate speeds of 30mph plus, and had little rollover strength. The DS suffered significant intrusion and collapse in a major impact, despite the rigidity of its lower floor pan punt or caisson.

This was the DS's secret for years – with DS experts and enthusiasts all reacting angrily to the discussion or suggestion of alleged weakness in 'their' car's structural performance. Such 'heresy' has been long denied, but today, even the French DS experts admit to this part of the car's 1950s' design context.

The true Citroën DS expert knows full well that the car was lacking in this part of its design – but the truth is so too were many cars of this era, as were many cars of much later years when car manufacturers knew more about structural safety and had less of an excuse to avoid the issue.

Seen from the present, the failings of the DS body in crash terms may seem concerning but this is a view from hindsight – back in 1955 few carmakers knew about or practised car-crash safety. It would

be wrong to condemn the DS unfairly given the context of its time, but the hard engineering facts are that its method of body construction was in terms of crash performance, a learning experience. When the Rover Company latterly used such a base-frame construction with non-stressed body panels for its P6 car, it went to great effort to reinforce and integrate the main body support and cabin 'cage' into the structure.

The DS enthusiast who denies the DS's structural factors – and many still do – only serves to undermine their own expertise and opinion. Indeed, the issue was publicly demonstrated in 1968 in the London–Sydney Marathon rally when even the rally-reinforced DS, crewed by Bianchi/Ogier, had a high-speed offset frontal impact in Australia and despite the fact that the other car involved was a short-fronted Mini (much smaller and lighter than the DS, with a differing mass), the DS suffered severe intrusion from the smaller car's impact. The DS's windscreen pillar/bulkhead folded backwards into the cabin, trapping Bianchi.

The Mini was of course, obliterated, but the collapse of the DS cabin at the crucial A-pillar/bulkhead mid-point was a salutary episode – especially given the lighter Mini it crashed with; the Mini

The very distinctive rear-roof coronet or trumpet rear lamp holders. This example is neither chrome/polished, nor fully integrated into the entire length of the roof rail's chrome trim. So that means these red trumpets are plastic and mounted on an early car or, unusually, fitted to a later car.
(Photo Author)

Earlier DS with lovely red roof and full-length integrated roof tumpets. Note wheel trims and windscreen sun visor – as seen on some tropical-market DSs. (Photo Author)

should surely have been little competition for the Citroën behemoth and its mass.

As recently as 2013, a DS in a classic rally in China suffered similar A-pillar and bulkhead intrusion after swiping a motorway guardrail. The A-pillar and structure of that car intruded over the sills and floor, far back into the front seating area.

DS *was* brilliant, but the suggestions that it was structurally excellent or 'rigid' and completely 'safe' in its main body, are way off the mark, but only the brave discuss the matter amid a sea of DS denial.

By 1960, the DS was established, known across the world and available in various specifications, not least the British-built Slough-specification cars. As trims and specification evolved, there was cast down the niched and the forensic type derivations that today fascinate the DS enthusiast and owner alike.

These included the differing ID and DS trims within each type respectively as a series of variations.

Of note, DS and ID saw such things as three different types of roof finish – from translucent to pigment to metal; a DS vinyl-covered roof, or a painted metal roof were also offered; four different types of roof trumpet types and trims, with three versions just for the ID; numerous bumper and valance options; a series of changes and types of rear lighting trims and types; numerous wheel trim changes; from 1965 a new five-stud wheel; several different dashboard designs and mouldings existed and the traditional British 'wood' dashboard of 1958–64 was a unique affair.

Before 1973, even the Pallas wore 'DS' badges on the C-pillar trim. Then the legend 'Pallas' was added. Pallas cars always had stainless steel-type roof trumpet finish and orange lenses. These two cars show off the differing door handle designs which saw flush-fitting handles applied from late 1971. (Photo Author)

The DS Men

These are the key men who created the DS:

M. Aligé	Michel Lefebrve
M. Allera	Paul Mages
Paul Baert	M. Maignan
Flaminio Bertoni	M. Meunier
Walter Becchia	M. Michel
M. Bouzinac	Jacques Né
Jean Cadiou	Raoul Henrique
M. Caneau	Raba
André Colin	M. Poillot
Henri Dargent	Roger Prud'homme
Louis Delgarde	Alain Paget
M. Dore	Claude Puech
André Estaque	R. Ravenel
Pierre Franchiset	Georges Sallot
Antione Hermet	Hubert Seznec
Pierre Ingeneau	* Bertoni's
M. Lachaize	successor, Robert
André Lefebrve	Opron would
	latterly restyle and
	develop the DS
	design.

Right: DS engine bay exposed with spare wheel removed for access. (Photo Author)

Below: Family fun in an early car: well-known Citroën restorer Mr D. Brownhill and family in their lovely 'oily rag' runner and all pumped up and on the go. Note the classic front-bumper design of the post-October 1962 type DS/ID. (Photo Author)

This car with dark plastic roof trumpets looks like a very early ID but it has square, not round, outer rear lights, and almost-black plastic roof trumpets (not brown) so it must be later car. Is it a rare ID Normale or a later ID19B? (Photo Author)

Deviations on a Theme

'Cats eyes' DS post-1967 headlamps and frontal panels seen in a typical Citroën advertising photo. (Citroën/Author)

DS or ID?

The DS as a car project was developed across two themes: the DS as the mid- to upper-market 'technology' car and the near-identically bodied ID19 as the lower market sector offering.

Initial problems in 1956 with the sealing of the pipes in the hydro-pneumatic system tainted the car's reputation at launch, but Citroën soon solved these issues. The glitch soon went away.

DS 19 soon became DS 21 then DS 23 – indicating increase in engine capacity. ID19 ultimately became the D Special and D Super (from 1969) – with a larger engine capacity and better trim.

All the focus and fame go to the DS and its glitz or bling trim and luxurious status in Pallas and then Prestige model iterations, and who can argue with that: yet what of the starker, more basic ID?

At its 1955 launch, even the French were astounded by all the technology in the DS – and the high purchase price.

So, to assuage those less than brave or rich and to keep its lower market sector customers happy, Citroën created a lesser-specification, cheaper DS and called it the ID. It was also termed as the ID Berline – Berline being the old French terminology for saloon.

DS 19 was the showstopper model of launch fame, but the ID19 came along as an idea in late 1956 and by mid-1957 had begun to sell. Of note, the ID lost certain aspects of DS design and the ID's engine was of simpler configuration and lower output. Both the DS and ID would soon be developed further with expanded model ranges and engine power ratings.

Some people prefer the simpler, austerity-model ID variant. Yet without

hydraulic steering and semi-automatic gearbox, without brown leather, chrome coronets, and luxury trim, and with a dull bare white resin roof, the stripped-out ID might have been the French taxi drivers' or French communists' Citroën of choice – to avoid any bourgeois DS imagery. ID was a third cheaper to purchase than a top-of-the-range DS. Poorer French farmers drove IDs as well as their 2CVs.

The late-1956-announced, 1957-model-year ID19 came as a very stark Normale-tagged trim level. It kept the hydro-pneumatic suspension, but not the ancillary systems and used a normal braking mechanism. Only a few hundred of the ID19 Normale – perhaps less than 400 – were ever sold. These cars were all-black, had bench seating in the front and rudimentary trims and plastic cabin and door trims and cards. Even the engine was cast-iron-headed and of just 62bhp output. Of note, the Normale had simpler rear wing panels and a cheaper steel bonnet. The C-pillar was also trimmed in basic metal. So, this really was the 'taxi'- or 'farmer'-specification DS on the cheap. A Luxe model was the next stepping stone.

We might argue that the true, mass-production ID came along from 1959 model year via the full sales launch of the slightly more luxurious Confort which sold widely for many years.

As early as 1962, Citroën added a second derivation of a conventional hydraulic braking system to the ID (not the fully integrated DS's hydro-system of suspension-to-brakes-to-steering-to-gearbox) and a fluid-powered steering option was an early 1960s offering. Yet DS experts are clear: the early ID did not get the 'button' brake pedal – it had a pendant pedal. ID lacked even a clock! Later IDs and D Specials did benefit from the full-house hydro-pneumatic braking set-up. But ID never received the hydraulic semi-auto gearbox of the 'proper' DS.

A very rare ID was the special Maitre version produced for provincial French officials such as mayors – many of whom were left-leaning and adverse to a glitzy DS limousine. So, Citroën produced an ID Maitre from mid-1959 for just under two years. This car had a glass partition to keep the chauffeur separate from the rear-seat dignitaries. Hardly egalitarian, but

Classic DS Pallas seen in serene repose. (Photo Author)

Christopher Wilson's lovely DS Pallas restoration in a fitting dark blue hue: a very late-model DS in all its perfection of form. (Photo Author)

1959 ID19 (Base Model) Technical Specification

Body: non-monocoque, non-stressed steel-clad subframe base unit: Plastic roof panel

Engine: 1,911cc, 4-cylinder in-line longitudinal inclined pushrod with later alloy 'hemi' head unit (replaced cast-iron head of early ID Normale); early production ID lacked a distributor.

Bore and stroke: 78mm x 100mm

Compression ratio: 7:5:1

Solex single carburettor

Max power: 66bhp (SAE) 4,500rpm

Max torque: 97.6lb/ft 2,500rpm

Max speed: 82.6mph

Transmission: 4-speed manual via single dry plate clutch (higher range cars with hydraulic semi-automatic gearbox)

Brakes:

Front: inboard discs of 11.8in diameter

Rear: outboard drums

Suspension:

Front: twin leading arms, self-levelling hydro-pneumatic; anti-roll bar

Rear: trailing arms self-levelling hydro-pneumatic; anti-roll bar

Tyres of Michelin 'X' design with differing (lesser) width to rear

Dimensions:

Track (front): 4ft 11in

Track (rear): 4ft 3in

Wheelbase: 10ft 3in

Length: 15ft 9in

Width: 5ft 10.5in

Weight (unladen): 24.22cwt

at least it was the ID not the flashy DS. Interestingly, these were alloy-roofed cars. Less than fifty were sold by Citroën.

The original ID engine had 62bhp then 67bhp, but soon received an 81bhp engine and then the 1,985cc engine of 84bhp which was tweaked across the 1960s to reach 108bhp. The later D Super 5 got the full DS 21 engine of 2,175cc/115bhp by 1972.

Approximately 751,000 IDs were built which curiously is more than the 500,000 or so true DS variants manufactured. So, the idea of a cheaper DS as ID, had been proven as viable.

DS 23 Injection Electronique – a legend framed. Note correct gold chevron badge. (Photo Author)

DS Delights

Above ID lay the reality of the original DS and its early trim variant nomenclature – of DS 19 then DS 20 and across Normale, Luxe, Special and Super derivatives. DS evolved through DS 19, DS 20, DS 21 and finally from 1972 into the 2,347cc (SAE) as a '2.3-litre' and the parallel fuel-injected version of that engine Type DX4/ DX5 at nearly 150bhp. Injection Electronique became the badge to have on the back of your DS – with the word 'Pallas'.

From 1964 in its defining Pallas trim, and perhaps finished in Gris Palladium metallic paint, specifically as an initial DS 19, then as DS 21, then DS 23 IE, the DS Pallas really did excel and expand into a true icon of French character that became famous all over the world. But other trim levels did not detract from the car's futurism or modernity.

Named after a Greek goddess as some form of alliteration, the DS Pallas was to become the defining DS icon; with extra sound insulation to the noisy engine bulkhead area, metallic paint, brown or black leather cabin trim, extra chrome ornamentation, more luxury and more power, Pallas became a DS symbol all of its own. This was not badge-engineering, but the creation of an almost-subset of the DS.

The true Pallas has chrome trim along the door–window line, delicate side-rubbing trims the length of the car and, of note, flat, brushed alloy trim on the rear C-pillar. Pallas was unique in its rear light and rear valance treatment using chrome. Throw in a sunroof, and the DS Pallas is just divine design encapsulated.

Yet we must not forget the DS Prestige model – an air-conditioned luxury limousine with a manually (then electrically) actuated glass partition in the cabin and lavish comfort in the rear: ideal for politicians and plutocrats. The Prestige was a Chapron-built car (see below) and you might even order a Pallas with Prestige accoutrements. Lower-level administrative functionaries could order or use a DS or ID that was more basic and known as the Administration Model.

Enthusiasts argue over the DS, and which is best, but we must cite the choices they make – such as, does a Pallas looks best in original upright headlamp design (perhaps with added podded spot lamps) or in post-1967 glazed visor frontal design?

Design in the Details

The intricacies of DS external design and its development across the 1960s can be best encapsulated by noting the following themes.

In the early years, e.g. 1959–64, the DS was subject to a number of design changes to the front valance, grille, bonnet airflow duct, bumpers and valances – all designed to improve airflow and cooling rather than just for styling's sake.

As early as 1959, Citroën started altering the shapes and dimension of the rear wings/fenders, not least to make it even easier to remove these panels to change a wheel. The rear wing was held on by one main bolt! It came with a special winding handle to remove it. All you had to do was pump the suspension up. Adding a jack support for safety was a good idea though, if available.

Original early DSs had exquisite long-formed coronet/trumpets that were part of the full-length roof trim, but the design was quickly truncated and even pre-1960 model-year DSs had short (red) coronet/trumpets, but there followed chrome finishes and paint-choice trims to match.

Three different rear taillamp designs and chrome treatments were used across the early decades of the DS.

Key identifiers for DS variants were the varying trim finishes applied to the rear C-pillar – from two grades of ribbed metal effect, also painted finishes, and latterly to the smooth aluminium decor of the Pallas type. Similarly, the coronet- or trumpet-type rooftop indicator light housings were subject to numerous materials and colours and coatings. The DS Pallas saw more chrome than lesser models. Many combinations of body colour, roof colour,

DS fronts old and later. Note vents in front wing of upright headlamp car, post-1967 restyled noses behind. (Photo Author)

The crowded engine bay with the spare wheel mounted to the fore – adding impact absorption but restricting airflow cooling effect. (Photo Author)

coronet colour and C-pillar trim were offered.

DS modellers and enthusiasts should note the vents cut into the front wings of 1959–62 model-year cars that were added to improve underbody airflow and reduce ambient temperatures.

DS model variant badges were in silver/metal finish but the nicest Citroën double chevron marque badge on the boot/trunk lid was a smart gold affair and looked even better on dark blue or black-hued cars.

In 1962, changes were made to the bonnet, front wing/fender-to-headlamp panels and designs. From later 1962, the cars had vents, new headlamps and new bumpers fitted.

The original plastic/glass-fibre roof in the ID series was unpainted, yet the DS roofs of such material were coloured. By 1963 the ID roofs were pigmented in their synthetic material by a white colour which gave a much nicer finish that was also less translucent than the original roof moulding. Herein lay the myriad of roof colour options seen on the ID and also the DS. A series of roof-to-body paint colour options were created. Some trim levels offered only a white roof, whereas others offered a body colour roof (as in the later D Super and Super 5), or the option of a contrast to the bodywork paint hue. Certain Pallas models had a vinyl roof covering. The DS was, of course, also to see roof colour options across the incredible number of paint and trim combinations.

In 1967, the DS was refreshed with a new nose that incorporated a slant-angled and faired-in design that saw four powerful headlamps set behind sloped glass covers that led into new front wing/fender shape: revised bumpers and revised interior designs and trims really did create a different type of DS, yet one no less dramatic and, in fact, more so. The etchings on the headlamp glass visors led observers to assume that these were heating elements, but they were not. However, a pair of the inner headlamps did turn with the steering to see around bends (only fitted when linked to power steering being present).

The new slanted-front DS was known as the 'cats eyes' look; people also referred to headlamp 'visors' and the style stemmed from new Citroën chief designer Robert Opron's work, but might also be traced back to Citroën sketches by R. H. Raba and J. Nicholas.

A very interesting range of modified fascia/dashboard designs were used across the DS's life (three main dashboard versions used) but it was Bertoni's ellipsoid original that remains the evocation of a starship emotion. As early as 1962's model year, a new, more Americanized dashboard of cowled design debuted. It was less pure in design terms, but more fashionable. It would be 1969 before the final, third dashboard design featuring round dials for the main instruments and new switches, entered the DS cabin design.

Perhaps we can say that the smartest DS was the Pallas trim level with all its chrome work, side trim strips and luxury seat covers and cabin trims. In the right metallic hue, it still looked like a 1970s spaceship – from a car design launched in 1955.

American DS specifications were complex and expensive to engineer. Significantly, the glazed headlamp visors of the post-1967 DS restyle were deemed illegal under safety legislation and the US-specification cars were devoid of these stylish lens covers. It rather ruined the effect not to mention the frontal airflow.

Legislation covering door locks, bumper-impact and emissions, all created expensive-to-engineer problems for the

A wider view of the DS engine bay. Citroënistes might not be so sure about the German battery though. (Photo Author)

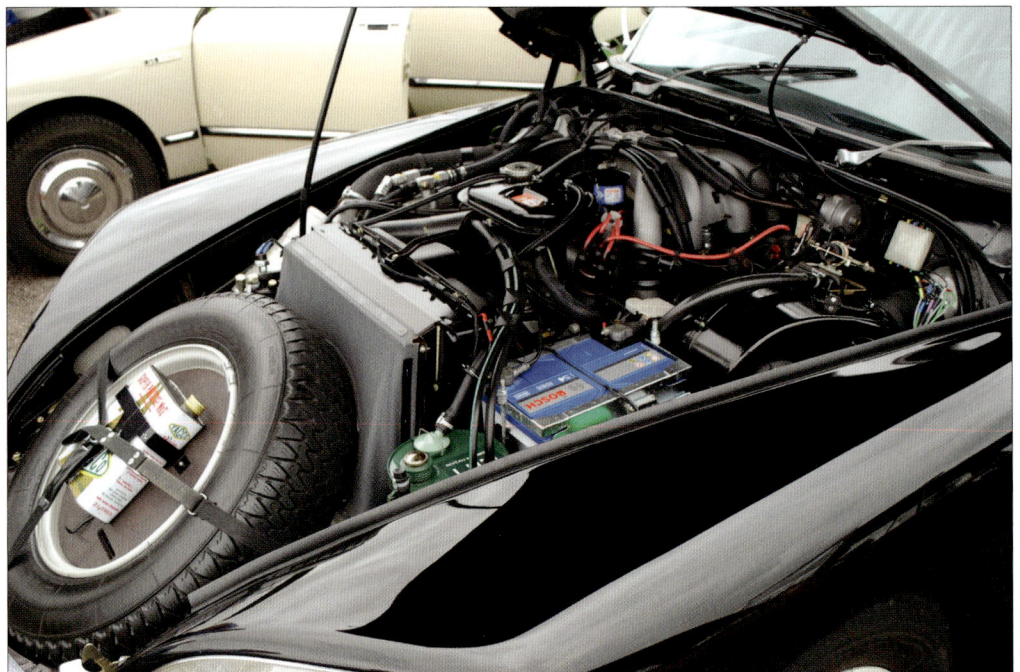

American DS and these costs were to signal the end of the DS in America. The front seats had to be re-engineered to take large headrests for American occupants – such things at that time being rarely demanded in Europe.

Laminated windscreens, tinted glass, 12-volt electrics, air-conditioning, a better radio, luxury seat trim, headrests, extra front indicator lamps – all these were American market specialities, as were unique model trim variant names such as DS Grand Route, DS Aero Super, and DS Citro-Matic (semi-automatic transmission). De Luxe and Comfort seem somewhat prosaic in comparisons.

Citroën America made many local changes to the DSs imported into the USA and these cars provide the DS enthusiast with a niche all of its own. Of interest a proper torque-convertor automatic gearbox

of Borg Warner Type 35 provenance was intended to be offered on later DSs bound for the American market circa early 1972 but, as an expensive option, the idea did not apparently take off.

Beloe left: Golden chevrons – the symbol of Citroën. (Photo Author)

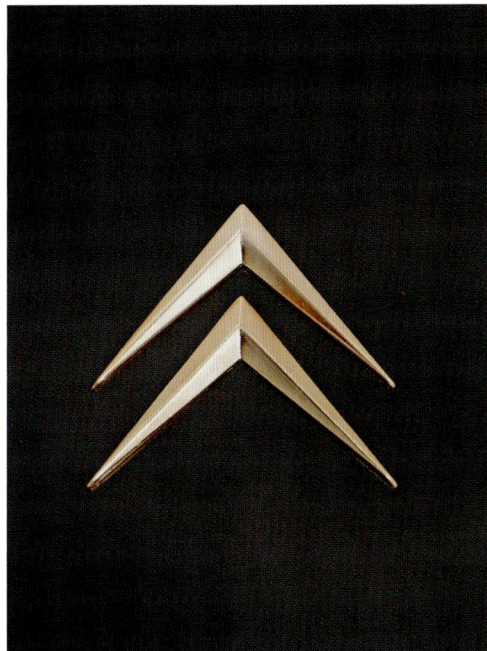

Above right: DS 21 in blue shows off the tail design of the DS and heavy curvature of the expensive-to-manufacture rear windscreen. (Photo Author)

Left: Earlier car with the telltale chrome strip beneath the bumper and pre-1962 bumper and front grille surround design. The headlamp illumination lights on the upper wing were also discontinued at this time. (Photo Author)

A last-of-the-line right-hand-drive ID-basis car as a D Super 5. This official Citroën model, announced in July 1972, was a variant that mixed the ID Super specification with the 2,175cc engine and five-speed gearbox from the DS 21. Note the rear lamp design changes of this French-built, 1973 British-registered car. (Photo Author)

Right: Seen from a different angle, this revised-styling car of the late 1960s is in left-hand-drive form and looks decidedly French in its non-metallic hue and contrasting roof. (Photo Author)

Below left: The stunning interior fittings on a mid-1960s DS. This is the second dashboard style post-1964, with duo-tone colouring and with linear-strip speedometer and flush switches.

Below right: The same interior with its two-colour style; after 1969 this type of DS dashboard was a cheaper, all-black specification. (Photo Author)

Top left: Red roof and red seat rim on a stunning DS. Note the very thick sills for safety, but the very thin B-pillar and its external sill-side mounting. (Photo Author)

Centre left: This is the British (Slough-built) version of the second dashboard moulding in right-hand drive guise with round dials of Smiths instruments type. (Photo Author)

Citroën simplified the dashboard experience with a new three-round main dial, black-finished, 'universal' type of dashboard which reduced production costs significantly. It was simpler in design and style and a single-colour. The D Special debuted this dashboard in 1969 but it was soon seen on the Pallas. (Photo Author)

The original front door armrest design lasted into the 1970s, trimmed in duo-tone colours. The door tops were to become fully trimmed (without bare metal) on most later models. The Pallas level of trim saw the use of leather-covered seats, and also featured the option of the newer 'Jersey' synthetic velour seat material in a pleated design post-1970. (Photo Author)

The extended-wheelbase DS estate and its unusual roof design (Photo Author)

The estate-car body significantly altered the DS design language. It also needed extra reinforcement and thicker metal gauges to carry the loads. The roof had a very limited weight-carrying capacity due to the very slim roof pillars. The vertically aligned, circular rear lamps were subject to several modifications. This one has reversing lamps that were included after the 1972 revisions.

A lovely late-model DS Break or estate seen in a rich blue hue. Note roof rack and large door mirrors. (Photo Author)

Estate Car DS

The first DS/ID estate car or 'Break' (a French term and not misspelt from the American/British Shooting Brake estate car terminology) was announced in 1959 and sales took off in late 1960 for the 1961 model year. Of interest, the DS estate was built for Citroën by an external contractor who extended the standard DS saloon and re-engineered the supporting structure. The roof pillars remained very slim indeed and even the tailgate frame hoop was slim-pillared. This might explain the low 80kg limit for the roof rack.

The fact that thicker steel (over 2.1mm) was used for the internal side members and rails, proved that more strength was required for the DS estate to carry its body and payload weights. With a longer wheelbase, base unit and body panel reinforcement and with some variants offering extra rear seating in the cargo area, these estate cars found massive favour for their long-legged driving abilities.

The estate's new rear-end styling was functional rather than pretty and turned the spaceship DS saloon design into a more obvious vehicle of normal usage. The variable ride height, as with all DSs, offered huge competency in difficult road conditions.

You could sleep, or party, inside a DS estate. A payload of almost 650kg seemed incredible and it was not just private buyers who flocked to the DS estate car: commercial enterprises used them and van-type derivatives, and even one with six wheels and an extended wheelbase was manufactured. From ambulance to repair van, DS estate was king.

The key models were Break, Familiale and Commercial. In Britain it was of course the Safari.

The Break, like the saloon, was manufactured from 1958 to the end of production in 1974 but with the last cars being right-hand drive models built in April 1975. The BBC used DS estate cars as camera-mounts, notably for following horse racing. The last DS estate car ambulance variant was built in 1976

British DS

Citroën had opened a British facility in London in the 1920s, and then moved to Slough in 1926, and had firstly built pre-war Citroën cars from kits of parts and then cars from its own Slough production line. The same was true of the 1950s/'60s Slough-built DSs which reflected the French variants except for the conversion to right-hand drive.

But sourcing over 50 per cent of the British DS's parts created some rare Slough-built specification differences – not least the special British-market dashboard design. From radiators to leather trim, tyres and even local paints, many parts of the Slough DSs were British supplied. The most notable British-built DS iteration was the DS 19 M variant which uniquely deviated from the French model line-up.

Of note, the British market saw a DS Executive as an official brochure-status variation of the DS and this was effectively a DS with an internal divider partition as seen on ID and DS Prestige variations in France. A radio-telephone fitting was an option.

DS 19 M was a non-automatic or manual gearbox 'mechanical' variant that rather quirkily did offer the other aspects of hydro-pneumaticism – via steering, brake and suspension – that the basic and original ID version of DS had not.

DS estate cars – known as the Safari (and the rarer Tourmaster) in the UK – were also Slough-built and offered with unique, local-content specifications and paints. The Tourmaster estate featured a revised rear-seating layout which offered full seating, or staggered seating with adaptable cargo space where the middle row of seats (of the three rows) could be removed. A large chromed roof rack was standard fitting.

The author's grandfather was one of the early customers for a Slough-built, British-specification ID and it had the rare wooden dashboard and leather seat trim of British origins; very few such cars remain extant today.

British-built DS cars were exported to the British Commonwealth and Dominions and of course parts were supplied to build DSs in Australia. After all, in Australia the Traction had been marketed as the 'British Citroën'! Just under 9,000 British-specified and framed DS/ID cars were born at or from Slough prior to cessation of DS manufacturing at Slough in 1964, yet French DS bodyshells were imported to Slough for completion, up to 1966.

In all, 6,737 DS were British-built for the British. A further 1,933 were exported from Slough.

Today many DSs survive in East Africa, Zimbabwe and South Africa where they were exported or locally built up from various levels of 'kit' components in local factories. Citroën France set up DS production in Australia and South Africa – not Citroën UK.

South African DS building from part-built or CKD (complete knock-down) packs imported from France began in the early 1960s as right-hand drive cars, but some left-hand drive cars were also created. Over the next decades, DS would be built in several factory locations in South Africa (ultimately in Port Elizabeth) and some experts insist that some were built in what was then Rhodesia from CKD packs rerouted into the country to avoid the sanctions imposed upon Rhodesia by the British government. Salisbury (Harare)-built DSs were real and the author has inspected and driven them in-country. Extra welding and reinforcing fillets were added to such cars, as was local trim

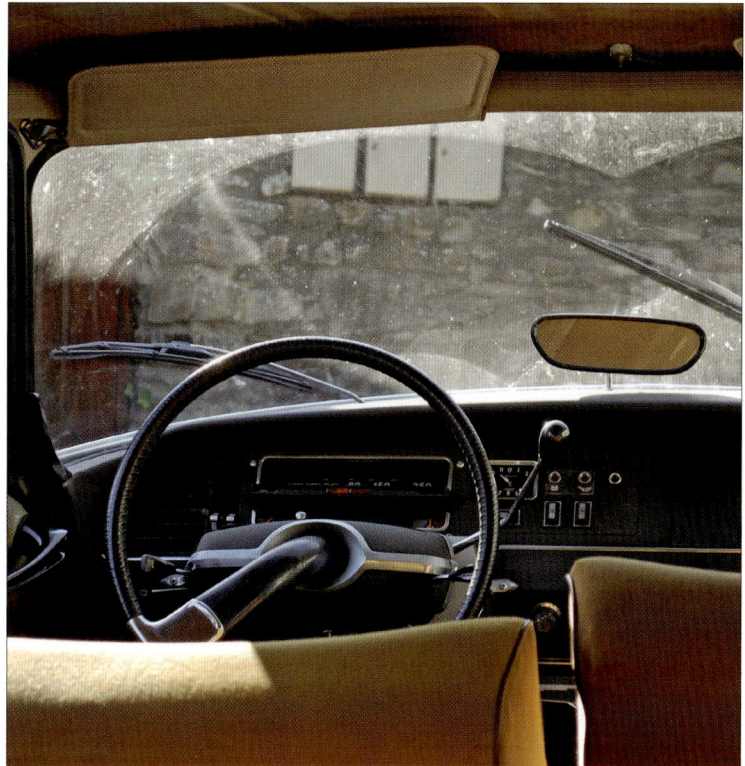

content and paintwork – often using British Leyland paint! DS manufacture in South Africa continued until 1975.

Australian DS

Australian DS production created unique variants of the model. The cars were built in the 1960s at Heidelberg, Victoria. These cars were given special, local-market nametags: the ID 19 Parisienne and the D Special Deluxe. Although right-hand drive and aping Slough-built specifications, there were many local market differences which were not seen in Europe. Australian cars were Paris (not Slough) sourced.

The Australian Citroën plant built 1,400 cars up until 1966. Locally sourced seat trims and an alloy roof panel as well as local 'duco' or paint were the key Australian-made ingredients. More welds and better dust sealing dealt with the demands of outback motoring. Latterly an oil-bath air cleaner helped 'up-country' cars keep going. Various manual and hydraulic gearbox specification DSs were created in Australia. So, the Australians got DS/ID with unique trims, better sealing and those 'Parisienne' badges. These 'Down Under' DSs were CKD or SKD (semi-knock down) as kit-pack-built cars with varying degrees of local build and content added at local point of manufacture or build-up. The earlier CKD cars were shipped straight from Paris (not Slough) and were much more basic than the Slough-built cars with all their added finery. The truth was that the complex DS suffered in rough and tough Australian outback conditions on corrugated roads and temperatures of up to 47°C.

Yet the DS became a fully built French import to Australia when the

Earlier estate car interior with the Mk 2 dashboard and, of note, the post-1968 seat backrest design. The trim option is Jersey Rhovyline material in a hue named Viel Or. (Photo Author)

A later-era right-hand drive DS dashboard with the revised steering wheel of 'safety' design. Still of DS style. (Photo Author)

This 1970s Pallas has had the lower dash section trimmed in contrasting colour that matches the seats and door cards.

so 'right' seen in a Thai, Malaysian or Balinese rice field? So, it is in Asia that an unknown legacy of DS remains alive and with a dedicated following. A quick web search will guide the reader to the work of Pierre Jammes and his dedicated DS in Asia researches – well worth a look.

Large numbers (over 97,000) of DSs were also built in Belgium at the Citroën factory at Forest near Brussels. Many such Belgian-built DS cars found their way to Africa and some to Asia. Some of the late-model Chapron-type DS two-door cars were finished in Belgium at this plant.

Connaught ID19 GT

Back in cooler Britain, a tuned-up British DS/ID with added performance and hydro-pneumatic mechanisms was marketed by the Connaught concern – an official British Citroën dealer that created an ID 19 GT with up to an extra 20bhp on tap through twin carburettor tuning and refining of engine components. This GT was five seconds faster to 60mph than a standard DS.

A revised engine with two options was offered by Connaught: a modified head with twin-Solex twin carbs, or a full GT Weber conversion. Raised compression, revised distributor, refinished internal engine components (ports, surfaces and manifold), revised cylinder head and, notably, twin carburettors, added to the DS drive. The Connaught ID GT could be purchased as a full-GT conversion, or the cheaper option of a partial, accessorised conversion package.

A revised braking kit with a Clayton de Wandre brake servo kit added to the car's stopping abilities.

The Connaught ID GT cars were advertised as the '100mph plus!' DS; for less than £150 the British DS owner would tune up their lethargic DS into a peppier performer. For an extra £78 Connaught would fit the DS's specification hydro-pneumatic steering pack to the ID GT. Reclining seats were offered but the thing to really go for was a Stirling Moss-branded wooden steering wheel – totally usurping the design of the Citroën single-spoke steering wheel!

Specials?

Special local-market modifications by importers, garages and tuners were one-off or ad hoc moments in the DS's after-sales life. If it was not fast enough, you could, like the French police, fit a supercharger to your DS. The French Robri accessories catalogue offerings allowed DS owners to personalize their cars with protective side-rubbing décor panels, badges and even a flash bonnet strip. Extra driving lamps were a popular fitting and so too were external windscreen visors in tropical climes. Numerous French and European accessories were marketed for the DS and made by the likes of GH, Robergel and

West Heidelberg factory closed in 1966: imported DS sales continued up to 1975 although the larger 2,175cc cars were not imported by Citroën despite the five-speed gearbox being available in Australia on the 1,985cc D Super. A total of just over 4,000 examples of the various DS models were sold in Australia.

The DS was hugely popular in Asia – home of former French colonies – and the DS Prestige variant owned by the last king of Laos, Savang Vatthana, is still resting peacefully in the sealed-off garage of the former royal palace of the old capital of Luang Prabang. All over Asia, old DSs in varying states of repair can be found puffing and wheezing their way through tropical climes in palm-tree paradise. Seeing a DS in such circumstances somehow makes the car's design seem even more incredible. How can a DS look

Sublime design: DS Pallas and essential stainless steel and chrome trim fittings. The tapering of the rear bodywork in three profiles is captured here. (Photo Author)

DS Pallas looking stunning in Gris Palladium paint but with contrasting roof hue. Timeless design genius. (Photo Author)

Sabolux. Garish after-market wheel trims and chrome strips for the bonnet horrified some DS purists.

Key DS Types 1955–75

DS 19	DS 21 E
DS 19 M/A	DS 21 IE
DS 19 A	DS S5
DS 20	DS 23
DS 21	DS 23 M
DS 21 M	DS 23 IE
DS P	DS 23 IEP

Engines

DS used a series of developed 4-cylinder engines. The original DS and its developed Sainturat-designed ex-Traction Avant 11D wet-liner three-bearing engine was replaced in 1965 with an effectively 'new' Becchia-developed 2,175cc five-bearing engine of heavily revised bore, stroke and torque curve. An alloy crossflow head improved the combustion process significantly and was latterly developed to 2,347cc with electronic injection. A few DSs were supercharged – notably for French police use.

The lobed and chamfered design of the DS and its aerodynamic sculpting is captured in this view of a much later DS Pallas. (Photo Author)

Top: The very rare glass-fibre, part-DS-based two-door 'Special', as a DB Le Mans Coupé Grand Luxe, was a second and later study on the Le Mans design by Messieurs Deutsch and Bonnet – the founders of specialist French aerodynamic marque DB. Panhard had also felt their design effect, prior to its purchase by the double chevron concern. Production continued (in the early 1960s) in very small numbers after DB spilt up and Charles Deutsch explored other opportunities. This is believed to be a post-1961 Bonnet-built car.
(Photo Author)

Centre: A modern yet less airflowed style was taken in one of the DB marque's less overtly aerodynamic affairs built upon DS underpinnings. The windscreen, glass, door aperture and some floor parts were all taken from the DS as a donor.
(Photo Author)

Bottom: The interior was a radical departure from the basis of the car. (Photo Author)

Key Main Engine Ratings

DS/ID 19, DS 20
1955: 75bhp (Type 11D developed as DS 19 engine), 1,911cc (3 bearing); very early cars lacked a distributor and relied upon coils and contact cams.
1961–5: 83bhp DA Type 1,911cc (3 bearing)
1965–8: 90bhp DY Type 1,985cc (5 bearing)
1968–71: 103bhp DY2 Type 1,985cc
1971–5: DY3 Type 1,985cc

DS 21
1965–8: 109bhp Type DX 2,175cc (5 bearing)
1968–72: 115bhp Type DX2 2,175cc

DS 21IE
1969–72: 139bhp electronic fuel injected Type DX3 2,175cc

DS 23
1972–5: 124bhp Type DX4 2,347cc

DS 23IE
1972–5: 141bhp Type DX5 2,347cc

This is the rare Pietro Frua-penned Bossaert GT 19 coupé of more obvious DS origins. (Photo D. Conway)

A DS Coupé/Convertible?

The Traction Avant had been made in two-door coupé and convertible or cabriolet versions, so why not the DS? Bertoni and Lefebvre had been keen on creating a two-door coupé type of DS – an upmarket car with the option of a soft-top or cabriolet version. Sketches were drawn up but went no further until Citroën relented after privately built Chapron DS cabriolet/coupé cars proved popular.

So initially it was left to outsiders, French specialist *carrosserie* (body) coachbuilders, to build low numbers of special DS designs – notably with two doors and soft convertible-type or removable roofs.

Yet Citroën decided to subcontract out the building of its two-door special DS and did so to the coachbuilder Henri Chapron who built that first private one-off DS coupé type. Chapron became the leading exponent of these cars. The Parisian coachbuilder first built fifty four-seater DS- and ID-based specials, most with two doors. These were best known as the Décapotable or cabriolet soft-roofed variants. Then came hundreds more of varying configurations and names. These were cars such as the Le Paris four-seater of which nine or ten were built. Then followed a special Le Dandy of tighter-spaced 2+2 configuration. Into the 1960s there followed the Concorde and Le Lemain four-seaters with square-rigged restyling. Chapron stylist Carlo Delaisse styled many DS re-imaginings and these included a further string of Chapron DS design including the Caddy, Lorraine, Majesty, Croisette and Palm Beach.

Chapron's two-door DSs featured revised metal gauges and localized strengthening in the upper side panels. Relying on the DS's sills and floor punt was not enough to tie-in the two-door body parts.

Special lights, trims, chrome fittings and colour combinations all marked out the upmarket nature of the Chapron DSs.

A Gris Imperial 1966 DS 21 Chapron-built Décapotable in all its original beauty. Note the added driving lights and 'aero' bumper and valance design. This may have been the last right hand-drive Décapotable supplied to the UK and perhaps one of only four produced to the late 1966 specification. Of note it has the Jaeger-type dashboard dials. This car is a later-type hydraulic (green) specification example. This wonderful car was restored using the original Chapron jigs and original parts and sold for over £100,000 in recent years. (Photo Author)

The Citroën-commissioned Chapron cars were given the title of Usine, or factory cars (*usine* being French for factory), to delineate them from Chapron's own private-build DS specials.

Chapron made the doors and base-pillars stronger and added double door catches with reinforcing plates in order to strengthen the DS's side panels. From DS/ID 19 through to DS 21 series, the two-door specials were an intriguing special-order story in the Citroën catalogue.

Despite production of official Usine DS coupé/convertibles stopping in late 1971, in 1978 a further one-off was built up from earlier 1974-built DS parts. Right-hand drive DS two-door specials had also been sold in the UK from as early as the 1963 model year and lasted nearly a decade on the market.

Over 1,300 Citroën Chapron DSs were built as well as over 100 private Chapron constructed examples. The best colours from the fifteen shades of paint for the DS two-door cars are arguably Orient Blue, Gris Imperial and Rouge Rubis. Red or tobacco-brown pleated leather seats had to be the connoisseurs' choice – after black of course. The engine to go for was the later 139bhp, 2.1-litre unit used from 1965.

A reroofed, long-wheelbase 2,660kg behemoth of a DS Présidentiellle for President de Gaulle was perhaps the DS conversion highlight prior to the SM conversions of the 1970s. The very last DS made was in fact a special DS 23 Cabriolet by Chapron and was built as late as 1978. This car was a special one-off using earlier manufactured parts.

Ricou et al

In 1959 a curious cut-and-shut DS two-door that looked like an awkwardly shortened DS saloon was produced by André Ricou on a shortened DS floor punt chassis. Two were built and Citroën used the idea as inspiration for its own two-door shortened rally car to be built by the Pichon Parat coachbuilder. In fact, Pichon Parat had also built a curious DS coupé with a new roof.

Less well known were the brief experiments into shorter DS coupés built in Marseille by Barbero.

From Hector Bossaert came the GT 19 – a pretty two-door DS coupé with unique Pietro Frua styling; just thirteen were built from 1961–5.

Today the two-door cabriolet-type DS built by Chapron is revered and of rising value. Some Citroënistes have built copies out of normal DS saloons and some have simply created soft-top four-door DSs. In Switzerland, a four-door DS saloon was manufactured as a conversion with a roll-back soft roof retained within the standard car's roof rail and pillars. These cars are extremely rare but easy to spot due to the non-standard roof contours.

The DS in Motor Sport

The DS was, despite its size, a strong rally car and under René Cotton's management the official DS rally cars competed in everything from the Monte Carlo Rally, to the London–Sydney Marathon, and the RAC Rally.

A DS won the 1961 and 1963 Tour de Corse and the 1000 Lakes Rally in 1962. DS won the 1966 Monte Carlo Rally in strange circumstances by inheriting the win after the British Minis were disqualified for a technical infringement. Much argument followed and the bad publicity caused Citroën to withdraw from FISA events.

The DS rally team had Henri Toivonen as its star; other DS conductors were celebrated writer Paul Frère as well as

Later-model DS as a convertible pressing on with four up. Sheer DS soft-top motoring.

The stubby short-wheelbase Ricou DS coupé. Two were made but Citroën was inspired to create its own short wheelbase DS rally car. (Photo Author)

René Trautman, Lucien Bianchi and Paul Coltelloni. Various privateer and dealer-supported DSs competed in events in Europe, Africa and Asia.

Godfroy's DS Genius

The enduring appeal of the DS as a special with a soft-top roof or a removable hard-top roof saw a remarkable exercise in 2015–19 when famous French industrial designer Gerard Godfroy created (with coachbuilder Christophe Bihr) a new, DS-based coupé of stunning elegance and scaling. His 'Grand Palais' pillar-less two-door design looked better than any DS coupé ever built and although a one-off, saw immediate demands for copies. Godfroy channelled Bertoni, added his own talent and made a DS beyond beauty, something world class in design terms: Godfroy also categorically stated (to the motoring media) that his reinforced version was much stronger and safer than the original DS with its propensity to 'come apart' in a crash. So spoke a French expert.

DS Timeline: Model Development and Special Cars
- 1955: Launch car with first frontal air vent/bumper/valance design.
- 1956: DS 19 fully launched, made until 1967; ID 19 announced October 1957.
- 1957: DS: Minor trim and front valance changes; variant ID 19 models with lower specification introduced with manual gearbox, no power steering and 63bhp engine.
- 1959: Break estate car body launched as five-seat estate and for 1960 as seven-seat Familiale; branded as Safari in UK from 1960.
- 1960: Specially built Citroën-branded DS convertible launched after Chapron's initial private venture conversion.
- 1961: Trim revisions and changes to estate car paint and roof schemes.

A DS on the Monte Carlo Rally. (Photo Citroën)

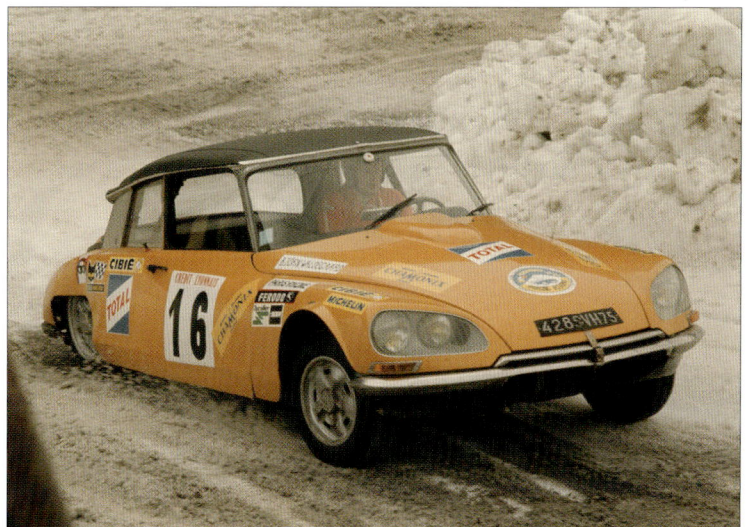

- 1963: Second version of revised frontal design and radiator aerodynamics; new dashboard design.
- 1964: Trim changes and dashboard switchgear revisions; first Pallas iteration; ID dashboard changed to DS-type dashboard design and trims.
- 1966: DS 21 launched and made until 1972; 2,175cc engine of 109bhp until 1968, then 115bhp carburettor unit; from 1970 with Bosch D Jetronic fuel injection giving 139bhp.

The official Citroën-sanctioned short wheelbase two-door DS rally car driven by no less a rally driver than the famed Björn Waldegård. Note bonnet vent exit bulge to spread warm air onto the windscreen to reduce winter freezing effect. (Photo Citroën)

Right: A near-standard DS seen at a checkpoint on the 1959 Monte Carlo Rally. The leather bonnet-retaining strap was a good idea. (Photo Citroën)

Below: Replacing the DS was a near impossible task. This shot shows off some styling ideas tried out in the Citroën design centre. From such draft ideas came the Opron-designed CX launched in 1974, itself a triumph of design and a special car in its own right.

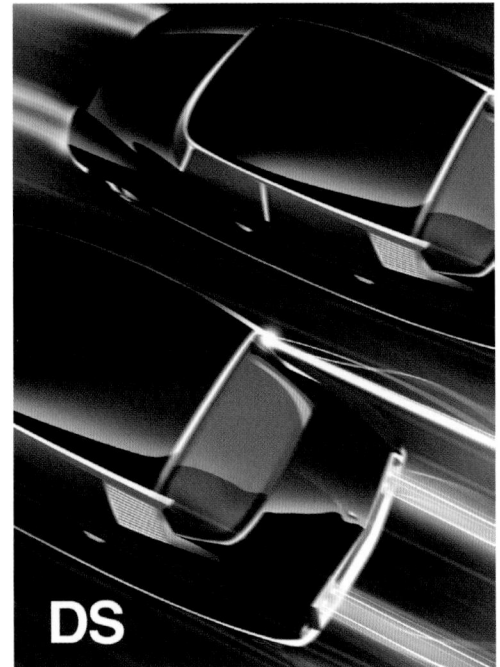

A DS at speed as captured by auto-artist Russell Wallis. (via Author)

- 1967: First major DS restyle (but as third styling variation) with new 'cats eyes' headlamp design and self-steer lamps; revised dashboard design.
- 1968/9: DS 20 revised engine; ID 20 1969 model year only; IDs have black dashboard treatment; fuel injection on DS 21 as production first; the 1,000,000th DS car type built (includes ID).
- 1970: D Super launched to replace the ID 20.
- 1972: D Super 5 uses DS 21's 2,175cc engine and five-speed gearbox. Revised dashboard and steering wheel for power-steering cars from 1972 onwards as highlights of the Pallas Injection Electronique years; fabric sunroof often fitted.
- 1972/3: DS 21 replaced by DS 23 with engine of 2,347cc with 124bhp in carburettor or 141bhp DS 23 IE fuel-injection specification.
- 1974: All-range DS production closes, except for some saloon and estate models.
- 1975: Final 770 saloons and 75 estate cars built; production ceases after worldwide total of 1,445,746 units built, as cited by Citroën.

- 1976: Final ambulance conversion built.

Over 1.3 million DSs were built in France and just under 125,000 externally. Total number of French factory-built across DS/ID range cited at 1,330,755.

DS was replaced by the CX from the 1974 model year and the last few DSs of 1975 signalled the end of a truly unique chapter in car design and automotive history. We can lament that it never got the advanced engine to match the rest of the car, and we can regret its passive safety challenges – in the context of their era – but we cannot ever forget DS and its sheer brilliance. Today DS remains a true icon and an act of daring that today's collaborative design-by-marketing would never allow. DS was no dinosaur; DS was pure genius.

A possible DS reinvention yet avoiding retro-pastiche? The author as an industrial designer made this design draft sketch of DS inspiration for a new DS. (Author)

Above: The DS seen with its replacement, the C6, behind. After CX came the XM, but there was a long wait for the C6 in an attempt to recreate the DS legend in a modern context. (Photo Author)

DS at rest in one of the rare rouge hues offered by Citroën: is that Rouge de Rio or Rouge de Grenade? 'DS' (not Pallas) on the C-pillar and non-flat door handles date the car's provenance. (Photo Author)

The essential and unadorned design elements of the early-series Citroën DS (19) circa 1956–59 are captured by automotive artist Russell Wallis in his dynamic rendering of the car's styling and design language. Note the covered rear wheel and the way in which the bodywork in the bonnet to windscreen area curves around to feed smooth airflow off the front of the car. The windscreen wipers are also shrouded. The pigmented-type synthetic roof panel in an early pre-1959 finish is also detailed – framed by the steel chrome-effect cant rail and coronet or trumpet rear roof lamps. The front valance includes the airflow-angled plinth for the registration plate. The chrome strip below the bumper means the car is a DS not an ID. Full-width wheel trims are not, however, fitted in this early specification. The C-pillar is smooth-finished and lacks the later flutes that were applied. The paint colour was the rare 1958 hue of Gris Mirage (AC142). (RJWDesign)

Pale beige was an unusual but long-lasting colour for the DS and its ID derivative. Of note, this DS 19 car has black rear C-pillars which were fitted to base model cars, certain special models for local authorities, the military and diplomats, and to the VIP Présidentiellle series cars. Full-size wheel trims and revised (post-May 1958) rear lighting frames (without the early red reflector strip) on the lower rear wing line show the subtle differences that were worked into the range by Citroën. This car has the B-pillar parking lights and no rubber overriders on the bumpers so the specification is circa 1959/60. However, the whitewall tyres are different! (RJWDesign)

After 1962, Citroën changed the bumper and front valance design for better cooling and airflow. Of note, small inlet vents were added below the headlamp units to admit more air into the engine bay to cool the engine as well as the hydro-pneumatic system fluid. Note the change to the bumper shape and the inlet vanes either side of the main central grille slot above the bumper – as well as differences to the under-car vents. The black roof colour seen with beige paint is somewhat unusual and more DS spec than ID spec. A lack of driver's door mirror is of note. Allied to the rear C-pillar design and the indicator lens type, this car is typical of an early- to mid-1960s DS. Gris Kandahar (AC133) was an ID colour but also seen on rarer DS choices. (RJWDesign)

After Henri Chapron privately pioneered the idea of a two-door DS convertible in 1958 with his DS Croisette, Citroën commissioned the factory or Usine series of such cars from late 1960, not least with a Chapron construction contract from Citroën. The very strong floor and sills of the DS meant that removing the car's roof (a non-structural item), caused little negative effect to the under-chassis, although some stiffening fillets were to be added. Paradoxically this 'proved' the strength of the DS's lower floor pan and sills, but also did likewise about the 'weakness' of the upper and floating panel body structure. Here can be seen the DS/ID Décapotable in the rather appropriate Bleu Royal (AC619) paint finish. Buyers preferred natural leather colour or black leather seats. The added driving lamps in their pods are rather stylish: of interest, Belgian and Dutch market cars had a differing headlamp trim type. Note the chrome trims to the rear wheel spats and the rear indictors mounted on the rear wing line. (RJWDesign)

Blue was not offered as an DS/ID colour until after mid-1958 with Bleu Turquoise being the first. For 1959, there were three new blue colours offered – Bleu Nuage, Bleu Delphinium and Bleu Nuit being named. This basic car in delphinium with a black roof and Hellanca Rouge interior captures the unusual specifications that Citroën offered to complement the car's radical appearance. This car has the long-tapered stainless steel/chrome-effect one-piece rear coronets or trumpets. DS focused upon the shiny metal-effect coronets after 1958 – having been seen with coloured plastic coronets in the earlier cars: a shorter shiny coronet design was used across the DS cars from 1959. The IDs would receive a moulded plastic coronet of differing, tapered shape and, of note, ranging in colour from brown (up to late 1959) to dark red, and then a shiny metal finish in the 1960s. (RJWDesign)

The DS estate car or Break used a longer body (extended rear body) with a differing rear subframe and reinforced chassis punt. Announced in late 1958, the Break did not enter manufacture until late 1959. The self-levelling suspension was ideal for a massive estate car or load-carrier. The Break was sold as both the DS and ID, but the ID variant was deleted in late 1972. Prior to 1968, a two-tone grey roof was available, but later cars had an all-white roof and several interesting roof-rack designs. The car's derivatives included the Familiale, Safari, Commercial, Ambulance, A23 and the Tissier-built non-factory six-wheeled commercial van of massively extended proportions used as a bulk-carrier and courier vehicle into the late 1980s. This later car with revised door handles and the post-1967 front characterizes the true nature of the big Citroën estate car. (RJWDesign)

Post-1962 DSs received revised front grille/valance and bumper designs. Of note, extra cooling slot vents were cut in to the front wing line below the headlamps. Further vents were to be added to the front wings to try and aid engine and fluid cooling under the bonnet.

Adding driving lamps (Marchal type) in delightful pods did not detract from the frontal design. Technically they were Pallas-trim items but could be dealer-fitted to any DS or ID. These lamps were seen on the DS, and the Décapotable. They could also be fitted to the ID, notably seen on British-built cars. A later pod design smoothed the lamps into the front valance more neatly.

Glass-shrouded 'cats-eyes' or slant-front lamps fronted the new low-drag, front-wing panel design for the 1967 restyle. Drawing on sketches by J. Nicholas and H. Raba and styled into reality by R. Opron, the new lamps had neat vertical lines as design motifs but not heating elements as some suggest. The inner lamps could turn with the steering – depending on specification.

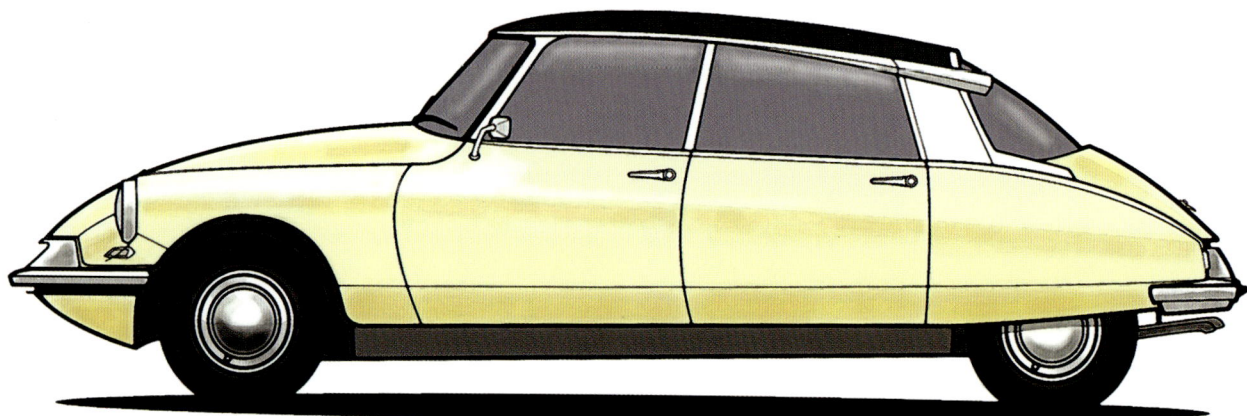

The classic DS 19 profile of post-1958 specification and depicted in the Jonquille (AC 305) colour. The C-pillar is smoothly finished and not fluted. The revised coronet or trumpet design is also evident. A black roof finish was an unusual choice. This pre-1960 car depicted is not fitted with the revised bumper design or the black rubber front and rear bumper overriders that appeared for the later post-1962 model years on the DS.

The car's classic DS frontal profile shows off the specification circa 1957/8 with the original bumper and grille/valance shroud design. The chamfered grille surround aped the front wing sculpting around the headlamps. The under-bumper vents were subject to several design revisions by Citroën. The horizontal slot vents under the front valance were eventually revised. The domed roof design is more obvious seen from the front. The front track was wider than the rear, hence the differences in the front and rear width appearances.

DS from the rear showed off its narrowing, tapered rear design elements. Pallas-specification cars had chromed trims around their rear lamp lenses. Reversing lamps were latterly fitted. One of the key areas of DS focus for the enthusiast and the modeller is the type and the design or the rear side lamps and their housings. British-built cars had round rear lamps. Early cars had elongated rear side lights, latterly to be replaced by square or round lenses with or without chrome framing. Italian-specification cars had unique square-shaped rear registration plates and a unique frame for them. Reflectors were also fitted to various DSs and IDs depending on their respective specifications and rear wing type. The upper rear indicator lenses were also subject to lens colour differences according to trim specification.

This pre-1962 model-year specification ID19 Confort in blue, shows off the earlier plastic rear coronet/trumpet design using plastic mouldings in a dark red colour and with a narrower, tapered shape with a unique chrome trim moulding where they joined the side roof rail trim. These coronets were to be changed from the 1959 model year. The C-pillar used a narrow fluted finish from this time but this was not the same as the later Pallas C-pillar fluted trim finish. A black roof would have been a rarer and later specification.

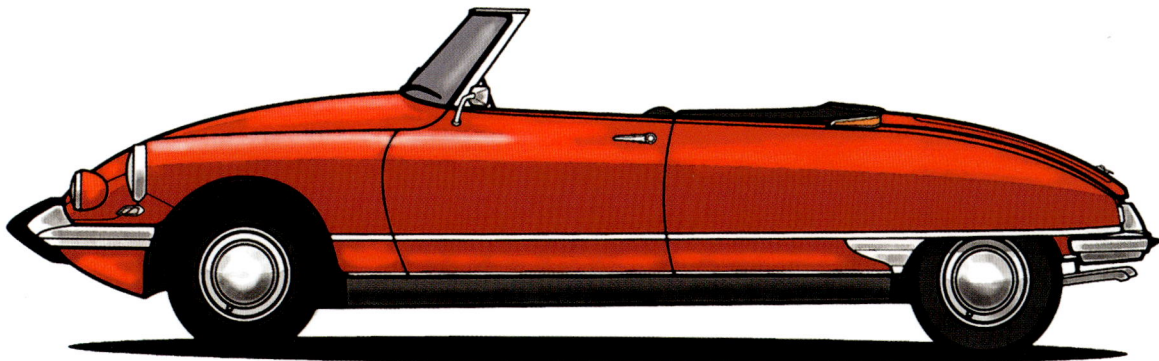

The roofless DS Décapotable of Chapron inspiration became the Usine DS convertible or Cabriolet. The very clean rear-deck design and integrated rear indicators on the wing line were very clever features. The specially built longer side doors also utilized double door locks to reinforce the side panel and locking integrity. The car also had two jacking points. Later DS Décapotables received the post-1967 slant-front restyle. Seen circa 1963, this car is in the rare colour of Rouge Carmin (AC411). Later cars would also see the fitment of the large add-on DS headrests which rather ruined the clean cabin line.

Prior to the 1967 restyle, the top-of-the-line DS Pallas featured add-on side rubbing strips, luxury trim, polished sill covers, extra driving lamps and the very attractive body-to-roof colour combinations. The trim plate on the C-pillar says DS and not Pallas (as post-1972) at this stage of the car's history. The C-pillar is satin/brushed aluminium finished and not fluted/ribbed as seen on later DS Pallas types. As depicted, the rich hue of Bleu d'Orient (AC616) with a silver-grey roof in Gris Nacre (AC095) really suited the car.

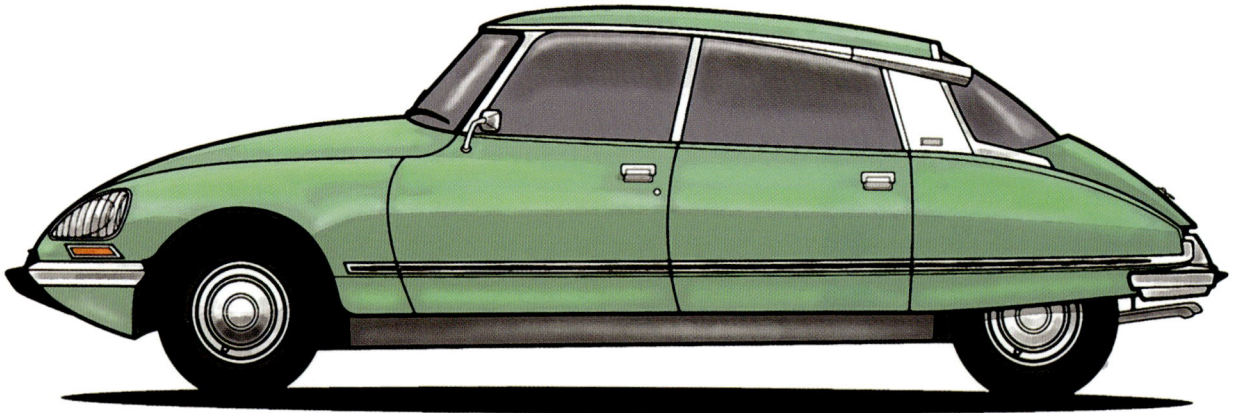

DS Pallas revised. The post-1967 slant front revitalized the DS and its global image; it also added to the car's design language and its presence on the road. More modern and brighter colours such as the metallic light green seen here were offered. Green shades such as Vert Illicinee, Vert Charmille, Vert Musicnee and Vert Argente provided a wide range of green paints for the DS. The new flush-fitting door handles indicate that this is a post-1971 car. Sill covers in stainless steel effect added to the upmarket aura.

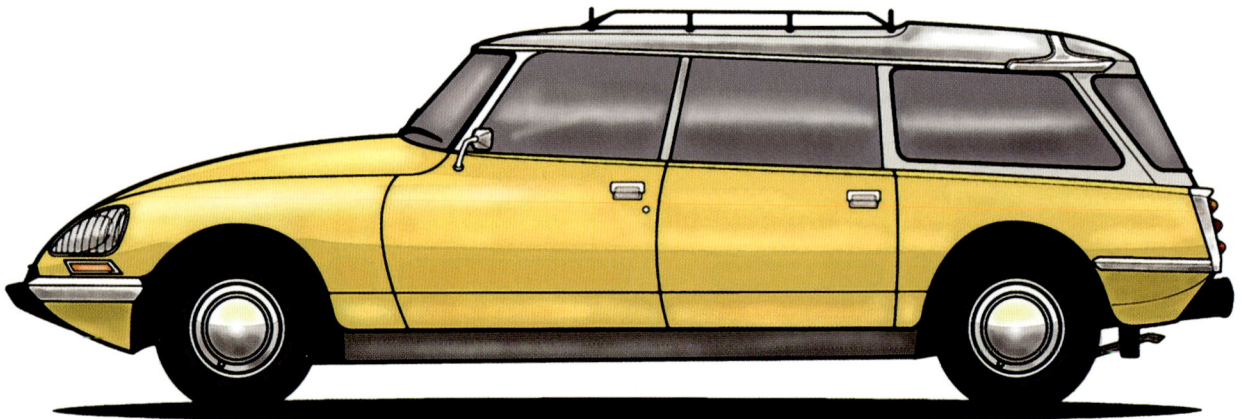

The DS 21/23 Break estate was world famous for its rugged abilities and self-levelling brilliance. Extra fold-down seats in the rear cabin created true six- or seven-seaters on such variants – the Familial had a row of folding middle-cabin seats (strapontins or jumpseats), which were not very comfortable due to their thin, upright design; the rearmost seats were more comfortable 'proper' seats but did not fold down. The Break could carry an astonishing near-650kg load, but the roof could only carry a low payload weight of under 90kg. Seven-seat and stripped-out commercial versions were offered, and the ambulance conversions were famous for their room and speed. The high-roof DS Break used for the ambulance was also utilized as a commercial type. Two types of DS ambulance conversions were offered – one being more fully equipped with medical and emergency kit. The 1970s late-life car seen here has the long roof rack. The rear lamps on the Break were subject to numerous variations according to market and model-year specification. The DS estate was known as the Safari in the UK before and after British DS production ceased.

Norev's masterpiece of metal die-cast is another early DS, this time captured in the launch colour scheme of two-tone springtime green and champagne beige roof and a 1955/6 specification. At 1/18 scale there is room for detailing such as the correct ribbed C-pillar to the rear roof and the accurate scaling and sculpture of the bodywork and aerodynamic styling – including the front bumper valance.

Die-cast & Modelling

NOREV DS 19 1956 Vert Printemps & Champagne 1/18 Model. Here lies the culmination of French model maker Norev's development of its DS models over the decades. Alongside the Norev DS 21, Pallas and the two-door convertible DS, as well as the estate cars and six-wheeled DS, the 1/18-scale DS offers a real capture of the defining brilliance of the DS.

This one is the 1956 launch version with bright springtime green (Vert Printemps) topped off with a beige-champagne (Champagne)-hued roof, both so typical of the bright shiny colours that Citroën, and also Renault, began to deploy in the 1950s. Of note, the car features the red plastic roof-mounted indicator housings known as trumpets (or coronets) – not the steel/chrome finish affair of differing shapes and dimensions that were fitted after September 1959 – except for cars in certain black and aubergine paint combinations which in 1957 used the metallized finish to the roof/indicator housing or trumpet. A shorter, stainless steel-finish trumpet would be used after February 1958 and on most DS variants after 1959 – interestingly, such cars had smooth-surfaced C-pillars in metal finish not the earlier fluted or ridged panel – and some panels were painted rather than fluted-finished.

Cast in metal with some synthetic details, this Norev DS 19 model sold out at its launch and is now, after just a few years, hard to find new and

unused. Of particular interest is the accuracy of the contours, body panels, scaling and details. Note the correct 'dome' curvature to the roof and the correct seep downwards. The windscreen frame brightwork, bumpers and even the special Michelin X-type tyres are all there for the discerning DS enthusiast.

Inside, the steering wheel and the DS's unique world first of a moulded synthetic dashboard have all been captured by Norev in this evocative model. Differences in the length of the rear wings/fenders (with a tooling change in late 1959 for the 1960s model years) and the lighting trim strips will be familiar to DS experts when the details of models are compared.

DS fanciers with an eye for the later DS types can also look to Norev for more sober colours and the later DS Pallas 21/23 series, as well as the convertibles and other DS types. Norev's 1/18- and 1/12-scale DS in die-cast are true delights and in the absence of a currently available 1/8-scale DS in metal and 'engineered' plastic from a major connoisseur edition, Norev's DS collection currently sits at the top of the collectors' market.

Two 1/8-scale DS models were previously available in 2013 and 2015 respectively. These were the Altaya/Pixo-branded DS 21 manufactured in Macau and the Premium-X-branded DS 21. Both were at 1/8 scale in metal and plastic hybrid die-cast and offered high-quality, high-cost models for the true DS collector.

In profile view, the tapered seep of the DS is evident. Note the correct, pre-1958 rear lamp trumpets or coronets in plastic. They were first displaced by long-form steel-finish coronets in cars of certain colours, and then replaced by shorter-form coronets in a steel/chrome effect finish from 1959. Belgian-, British- and Australian-built DS cars would have interesting differences in such details.

Seen from a lower angle, the nose prow is more evident with the bonnet/hood shape – as is the sculpted form of the early bumper and intake configuration. For the purist, only the whitewall tyres will raise concerns.

Rear-quarter view reveals the correct 1956 specification to the rear lower lamps and with the red insert to the side strake – which was deleted from the DS in early 1958. Note also the curved rear windscreen and trailing-side trims onto the upper rear wings/fenders from the C-pillar.

Apart from a small numberplate anomaly, this head-on view captures the sculpted front profile of the DS. In 1962, extra ventilation slots were cut into the panel around the headlamps. Note the telltale small lights above each headlamp which served to let the driver know the lights were working correctly.

DS was complex in the rear lamp and bumper panel. Several changes were made to lights, lenses and trims. After mid-1959, the rear wings/fenders were altered in shape and length and the rear reflector and side strake design removed and a new outer lamp reflector substituted. Norev have done well to capture this intricate rear lamp assembly so accurately.

Looking down on the complex rear detailing. Note the shape of the rear windscreen and the trim along the roof's rear edge.

The rear roof C-pillar was subject to several fluted or ribbed finishes, also a smooth and painted finish and in later Pallas cars, a smooth-stain aluminium finish. This C-pillar panel is a key area of gauging DS model accuracy.

A wider view of the rear end and its design. Note the correct boot/trunk lid release without handle. The exhaust outlet is also of note as it was latterly changed to a different design. Gold chevrons were the real deal on DS. No other Citroën brand name was obvious on these early DSs. Note the ribbed indicator/stop lens design. Later DS and Pallas models featured shiny metal trim to the lamp cluster, and white reversing lenses, respectively.

Norev even got the finish on the single-spoke steering wheel to a perfect scale detail. Note the frameless windows.

Seen through the aerodynamically curved windscreen, the DS's one-piece dashboard moulding reflects yet another aspect of the car's advanced design.

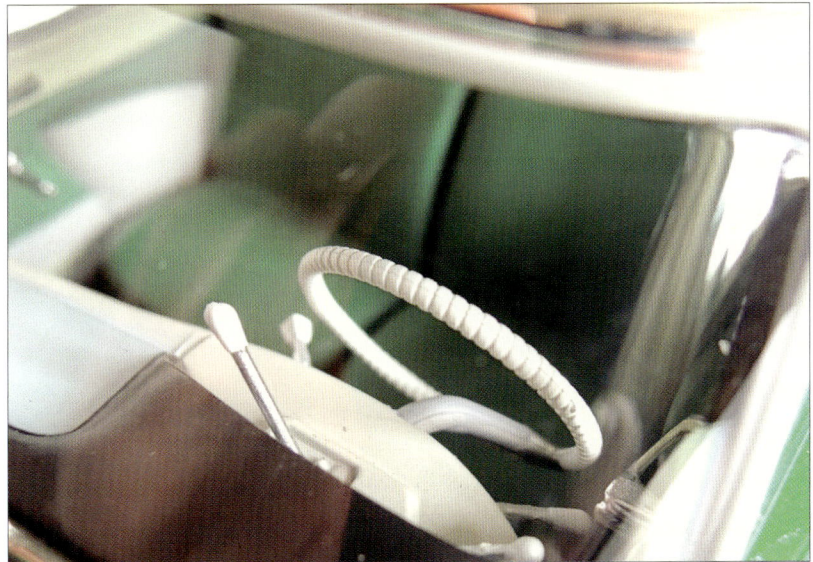

Front detail with the stylist Bertoni's original bumper and intake design – which would be improved upon in airflow terms by 1961. Belgian-built DSs had unique headlamp trim rings with slight cowls: here we see the original French-specification headlamp design. The ID variant often used painted headlamp trim rings – not chrome-type.

Seen from above, the tapering, biomorphic form of Bertoni's DS sculpture is captured. Note the narrower rear track.

DS Décapotable (Convertible/Cabriolet). Originally suggested and built in 1958 by Henri Chapron, then absorbed into a Citroën factory or *usine* production series from early 1961 (built to order by Chapron), the two-door soft-top Décapotable or cabriolet (and as a later hard-top coupé) DS variants are now seen as the top-of-the-tree DNA in the DS story. A right-hand drive version was available as early as 1962. The DS factory-commissioned cabriolet line remained available until 1971. However, Chapron built up to three more on late DS chassis in the mid-1970s with the last DS 23-based car delivered as late as 1978.

Norev produce these cars as die-cast models at 1/42 and 1/18 scale in fine detail as can be seen here.

Significantly, to create the cabriolet the boot/trunk line was altered, the indicators placed abeam the rear wing haunch, and extra strengthening added to the sills, door locking plates and locks and two jacking points (not one). The rear seats and, of course, the folding bonnet/hood mechanism in revised side panels, are obvious changes from the DS saloon; changes to the badges, trims, brightwork and other specifications are also evident. From announcement in 1960, to production from 1961 onwards, the DS 19, ID19 and on through the DS 21 to the 21 IE, the cabriolet, be it as a Chapron private-build car or a series-production 'factory' Citroën/Chapron car, oozed style.

The dark blue model shown here is in Bleu Royale and has leather *naturel* – perhaps the most sophisticated trim combination. Silver grey, as also modelled, was popular.

The DS in its die-cast forms has become the recent DS model movement with 1/18 scale being favoured at main scale. Norev's 1/12-scale models were soon snapped up as exclusive editions.

However, resin-cast plastic model kits for the self-build modeller remain very popular, not least because so many DS specification variations can be created.

The essential DS Décapotable or cabriolet/convertible. This Norev 1/18 DS die-cast is stunning and quite rightly finished in Citroën's dark metallic blue and light tan leather combination (see text for details). Note the side strips, sill plates and front driving lamps in pods.

Another Norev model of the DS Décapotable in silver-grey metallic and a maroon leather interior.

DS Décapotable at smaller 1/43 scale in red by Norev. Note the revised front bumper and valance design, meaning that this is a post-1962 type.

DS Pallas. Was this the *Déesse* concept personified? The DS in top-of-the-line Pallas trim was ultimately expressed by the DS 19, DS 20, DS 21 and D 23, notably as the electronic fuel-injected car with stainless-steel trims, luxury leather-lined interior and post-1967 in 'cats-eyes' slant-front styling revision. The car never received its intended larger engine of greater capacity with more cylinders, yet in fuel-injected form, DS Pallas symbolized the ultimate development of the concept from 1964 as the DS Pallas to 1975. Only the limited-edition Pallas Prestige version build in low numbers (with air-conditioning) sat above the DS Pallas, but the Prestige was designed to be chauffeur driven and had a front bench seat and a cabin partition in glass. Norev's die-cast DS Pallas is of a later DS with classic dark blue paint, silver roof and the sumptuous brown *naturel* leather interior. With opening driver's door and bonnet/hood, the model is well-detailed. The Pallas trim car has the smooth-skinned, brushed aluminium C-pillar – not the ribbed finish – and, of course, gold badging. Note the full-length side-rubbing strips, sill covers and bumper overriders in black rubber. This is the DS captured in style.

Ultimate DS? The post-1967 facelift slant-nose DS in wonderful Pallas trim as scaled by Norev. The revisions are obvious but note the smooth-finish C-pillar and side rubbing strips: by this time the production car's plastic DS roof had been replaced with a metal item across the ranges. Also seen here are the long-form roof coronets. Dark blue paint and tobacco-brown interior really looked good on DS Pallas.

Basking shark: DS captured by Norev in the metal in all its ultimate form. This colour is Bleu d'Orient, perhaps only matched for style by Bleu Delta.

Die-cast Delight & Resin Royalty. The first person believed to have produced an accurate scale model of a Citroën was André Citroën himself who in the 1930s commissioned pedal-car 'model' Citroëns in the belief that if children experienced his brand at a young age, they would buy a Citroën in adulthood. He may have been inspired by Ettore Bugatti's handful of similar-scale children's pedal-car versions of the Bugatti Type 35. It is reputed that George VI's children, Elizabeth and Margaret, both received Citroën pedal-cars as children.

Today the DS has a tribe of fans and many modellers across varying materials and scales: modelersite. com, scalecar.net, HobbyDB.com, scalemates.com, britmodeller.com, scaleauto.com and carcollectors-garage.com all provide excellent portals of DS model learning and commentary.

The DS as a car is now over sixty-five years old, which means that models of the DS have been on the market for several of those decades. The famous 1962 incident when President de Gaulle escaped an assassination attempt in his DS (with the car's tyres damaged) has been captured in model scale. The 1972-built Michelin tyre company's modified DS flatbed 'truck' with ten wheels formed the basis of an early DS conversion (it was known as the Mille-Pattes, or Centipede): this car and later DS six-wheeled conversions have also been modelled at scale.

A plastic die-cast one-piece DS was moulded by Norev, the famed French model carmaker, very early on in the DS's life, soon to be replaced by Norev's ever-improving die-cast metal renditions of the DS in scale. By the height of the late-1960s DS era, the DS was to be modelled as a resin/plastic self-build scale kit by French car model manufacturer Heller; Heller would also have a link with Airfix. Even Revell would produce a 2CV and DS model set.

There are collectors' DS models available across all its years and body types. Recent larger-scale releases from die-cast leader Norev have become instant collectors' gems and they sell out fast. Earlier DS models have become very rare indeed. These include such releases as the Norev Three-inch Line (which despite the small scale, accurately sculpted the DS) and Ligne Noire (Black Line). Older releases include Dinky, Atlas, Corgi, Rio, Majorette, Solido, Vitesse, Eko and Eligor.

Oxford Die-cast offer a British take on the DS at 1/76 scale. Of interest, Eligor produced a 1/43 scale DS 'Blake and Mortimer' special edition reflecting the comic series and a brown DS that appeared in it. Husky and Atlas (ex-Dinky) have all been brands that produced varying licensed versions of similar mouldings for small-scale DS models. Husky's DS Safari at small scale was very well detailed and cast.

Rio of Italy have produced several DS rally car editions as tribute to the DS's rallying history. These are now collectors' items despite small errors in their shaping accuracy. The Vitesse Models brand from Portugal (manufactured by Cinerius Ltd and now Macau-owned) produced a limited-edition 1/43 DS 19 Pallas in the late 1990s and several other numbered-edition DS diecasts.

Several 1960s and 1970s models were die-cast one-piece plastic mouldings of the DS. Intriguingly, Lego of Denmark produced a little-known one-piece HO-scale DS in plastic in 1965. This is now a rare collectors' item. Another rarity was a DS part-work build kit from a publisher that allowed the reader to construct a large-scale DS over many months.

Stelco Plastic offered a synthetic-cast DS and Tomte Plast issued a DS 19 Décapotable. Schuco of Germany have released their model of the 1972 DS Présidentiellle – the rebodied DS limousine used by the French government.

Above: A French rural diorama surrounds this DS Break estate car in *vétérinaire* specification as modelled at 1/43 scale by Atlas in its *petits utilitaires* range of commercial-edition vehicles.

Centre: The extended tail of the DS estate and vertical lamps are shown here at 1/43 scale. Observe the roof rack. A load limit applied to it. The tailgate is a two-part spilt design which was very useful. This model depicts an earlier French market car with the amber and then multiple red rear light stacks. Some non-French cars had red and double-amber lamps; others had later, white (reversing) lenses and, by 1972, all DS estates had lower reversing lamps and lenses. Establishing the correct lamp design and colour is vital for the serious DS modeller.

Bottom: This Atlas edition car is modelled with the suspension set on the high setting for rural use by its driver. Of interest, the car has the bright blue seat trim which instead of being of Jersey fabric, would likely have been Bufflon wipe-clean material as used on commercial cars.

Matrix produced a 1/43-scale DS hearse (to represent a DS estate car-hearse in full-scale production). Ex Mag Model Cars produced a DS 19 *Vétérinaire* (vet surgeon) estate with an interesting diorama as seen in this section. A bizarre 1970s DS model was the Corgi release of a BBC Magic Roundabout special edition featuring a modified DS carrying that programme's lead characters as modelled.

Politoys issued a DS Pompiers fire engine-specification-equipped DS, and we must not forget the six-wheeled DS platform rescue vehicles nor the six-wheeled DS vans used for cargo, documents and overnight newspaper delivery in Europe well into the 1980s and which have been modelled.

Bburago's 1/32-scale DS castings provided the enthusiast with access to the DS as a model but as with early Solido and early Rio models, there were some issues with capturing the DS's unique styling. Bburago's later models and the more recent Street Classic line-up have achieved higher detail quality. Solido released a more accurate white DS with a black roof that, although not overly finessed in detail, certainly offered the collector the DS as it was in mainstream use. Solido also released the 1/18 DS Presidentielle car complete with flag pennant and adjustable suspension and fold-back sunroof.

Eko's 1/87-scale DS was unusual: A DS estate car converted into a 'ute' flatbed type modelled by Corgi was a rare model and remains so. Majorette issued a DS ambulance. Del Prado Publishers issued a part-work-collection build 1964 DS 19 at 1/43 as a special-edition model in 1999.

Atalya of Spain have offered a series of DS die-cast models in varying finishes and levels of detailing across several decades. White Box produced the DS 19 in 1963 specification in die-cast zinc (and plastic) at 1/24. This model had opening doors and bonnet/hood and boot/trunk.

Heco Miniatures produced a 1964 DS 19 Chapron Le Dandy at 1/43 and the Chapron Palm Beach. Restart produced a rally-specification DS 19 at 1/43. Rallye-Miniature also produced a 1/43 DS rally car of drivers Trautmann/Ogier and the same tooling with decals for other driver pairings.

One rare DS model was the DS 19 model of about 1/24 scale with a small electric motor and a cable drive from a steering wheel-equipped hand-held control box. A limited-edition powered DS 19 model moulded in plastic with an armature motor was a rare limited edition, now highly prized.

More recently, Japanese model provider Ebbro have produced a good-quality DS kit in 19 and 21 variants.

The scales offered across the die-cast DS models range from 1/87, 1/43, 1/32, 1/24, 1/18, 1/8 and, in earlier years, 1/250.

The very rare Norev-edition model of a 1958/9 DS two-door short-wheelbase coupé (55cm shorter) by André Ricou was designed as a rally car and GT-type tourer. The Ricou cars were lighter and had tuned engines of greater capacity and could get to 180kph. Ricou drove one in the 1959 Snow and Ice Rally. Famous rally driver René Trautmann drove one in the Rally of Corsica in 1958. Ricou would also sell you a road-specification version of their car but only a handful of all the Ricou DSs were ever built. A British DS 'sports' conversion in a standard DS body was built and sold by Connaught Engineering in 1963.

Both Norev and Ministyle released DS Ricou scale models (in blue or maroon) – with Ministyle's being a version in resin cast. We might say that both the original Ricou and the models of it, captured its 'challenged' styling.

This Italian-made Rio model at 1/43 in die-cast metal is an East African Safari Rally edition and suitably decaled for drivers Pointet and Houillon. As you can see, the proportions are not quite right, but it is now a specific collectors' item.

Rio's models were always 1/43 scale and from the 1970s, models from Rio, like this DS rally car, found a ready niche amongst the enthusiast groups. It might be a little crude, but it is charming and very 'DS'. Rio also made a rare DS hearse model with an open rear deck.

Even at this scale, Rio offered an opening door and some level of interior detailing. Rio has now been restructured within the Italian scale-model producers and faces competition from Brumm Models.

Norev. It is fitting that French die-cast model maker Norev should lead the field with its vast range of DS models across several scales. Norev hail from Lyon – close to where Citroën and engineer Lefebvre did much of the secret development work of the DS. Founded in 1946, Norev's early model cars were, shall we say, a touch naïve, and modelled in the then new material of cast plastic using a Rhodalite compound developed by Rhône-Poulenc, the French chemical company.

Norev produced its first plastic DS model in 1958 and improved upon it greatly across several mouldings. The use of plastic and bright colours in Norev models suited its rendition of the DS well. Norev's first model to feature glazed windows was their own DS model.

Original Norev scales were 1/43 and 1/87, In the 1960s, Norev created a marketing brand called Ligne Noire or Black Line and in this series issues the Chapron DS variants. Despite being plastic-moulded, these were accurate precision-moulded items. Norev has nothing to do with 'no-revs' but is a reversal of the founding family's name of Veron.

It entered the metal die-cast era in the late 1960s. Strong competition for collectors' quality and well-rendered and accurate die-cast models already existed forcing Norev improved its detailing, scaling and casting.

Via various corporate iterations and changes, Norev has evolved and provides a stunning range of highly accurate DS models in two lead scales of 1/43 and the larger and more expensive 1/18 scale – it is here that the Norev die-cast DS story stretches across several mainstream and limited-edition collectors' series in many versions. A 1/12-scale Norev DS limited-edition model depicted the 1959 model year car. A Norev 1/43-scale DS Break in black and specified as a Radio/TV Luxembourg car is a rarer item now.

Of interest, Norev have accurately rendered the original Citroën paint hues and coloured DS roof combinations. As can be seen in the classic 1950s rendering of a green DS at 1/18 with beige roof, die-cast by Norev seen here, today's DS die-cast collectors' item model is the closest yet to the real car.

Right: Dinky (Toys) released the DS 23 Citroën in its own 1/43 small-scale series in the 1970s and had also released the DS 19, a police car DS, and other special editions. Dinky also offered a nice range of Citroën two-tone roof/body colour combinations of true DS provenance. French and Spanish Dinky DS editions were also manufactured. The rarest Dinky DS, especially the early DS/ID 19, now fetch large sums on the collectors' market. In the late 1960s, Husky produced a DS estate Safari at 1/43 with a boat attached to the roof rack.

Below: Solido have produced a series of DS models and this white DS with black roof as a 1963 car provided an affordable entry level into DS die-cast. Solido's 1/18-scale Prestige range included the D Super, D Special and DS 20 of the early 1970s.

DINKY TOYS   **DS 23 CITROEN**

With correct detailing, a rare black roof, the appropriate C-pillar panel and opening doors with a good interior all marked the Solido DS Berline as a worthy die-cast DS.

The contours of the Solido DS die-cast were accurate and the black roof added to the DS effect of a tapered and streamlined form by visually lowering the roof line. Solido also issued the model in taxi, rally car and police liveries/specifications.

DS Details in Focus

When kit-building the various DS iterations, it is vital to use accurate production car or production-specification restoration car details as reference material. The DS came in a myriad of specifications, colours, combinations and trim options and differences. Key model-making issues to be aware of for your DS build include:

- Correct rear C-pillar finish and ribbing as defined by model and year specification.
- Correct type of rear roof coronet or trumpet indicator housings and lenses according to specific DS chosen.
- Careful attention to roof and roof rail trim around front windscreen and car.
- Mid-B-pillar and specific finishes and lights.
- Appropriate badging types and colour use.
- Choice of relevant wheel type and wheel trims to trim and year specifications.
- Ensure correct front (and rear) bumpers and valances as appropriate are modelled.
- Ensure rear lamps and lenses are correct for type and year of DS modelled.
- Correct rear lenses and bulbs colours/types on estate cars; also, roof racks and interiors.

- Interior colour and trim materials correct for car and model year. Note three differing dashboard/fascia designs and further British-specific 'wooden' dashboard with revised instruments; Pallas specifications such as headrests, leather trim and more; differing interior trim materials and colour schemes.
- Engine bay details and hydraulic pump and pipes correctly modelled.
- Suspension setting as appropriate.
- Panel gaps, door shuts, door handles, glazing, headlamp rim trims, specific model-year vents and grilles.
- Wheel trims and wheel types.
- Sill panels, e.g. Pallas type.
- Correct door handles, hinges and mounts for two-door Chapron and Usine-type convertibles.
- Break/estate car, Safari specifications.
- Differences between French-, Belgian-, British-, Australian- and overseas-built cars in paints, models, trims and specification differences; US specifications vary.

The expert DS modeller will need to be forensic both in research and application.

Heller produced a self-build DS kit in moulded plastic early on and today, 1/43-scale Heller DS kits are still available in the model marketplace. Heller produced a new 1/16-tooling DS in 1980 and then created the two-door cabriolet Décapotable versions in 1982 (Heller Humbrol branded). Both these kits have been reboxed across the last three decades and as late as 2020 the Heller kit was reissued as a DS Berline starter-level model set. Heller's Normandy manufactured a 1/43 smaller-scale kit with twenty-six components and, measuring 112mm x 43mm when built, is still available (with recent Citroën branding) for the younger modeller.

Heller's 1/16 Grand Scale models include the original DS 19 and, of note, the DS Décapotable two-door soft-top. The Heller DS at 1/16 scale is 298mm long, 11mm wide and 91mm high – and when correctly constructed, presents a really accurate rendition of the early DS 19. Heller produced a DS 60th Anniversary DS kit edition too.

Heller of Normandy, France, have been producing DS models across several scales for decades and this box art belongs to the current entry-level 1/43-scale kit of the DS 19. Ideal for the younger enthusiast.

Model Kit DS in Focus

Starting from the 1990s, Japan's Ebbro model company has released many well-scaled kits and after some years, produced the current moulding of a post-1967 facelift DS 21 (slant nose) which is very well moulded and was licensed by Citroën. An earlier DS 19 upright-headlamp model from Ebbro remains very popular and is of excellent scaling, detailing and moulding. Only a little ex-sprue modification work is required with this moulding in order to reach high standards

What was really nice to see in the Ebbro DSs (also cited by some as Ebbro/Tamiya) was the correct DS badging rendered in gold, not just the silver script of other models. Gold badging really hit the accuracy button, as did the correctly graded C-pillar trims in ribbed metal (as opposed to the smoother finish of the DS Pallas specification.

Below, we follow an Ebbro DS 19 1956 model-year build in injection-moulded reality.

Key DS Paint Schemes of Note

Space does not allow us to list the entire repertoire of Citoren's vast array of DS colours, trims and combinations, but a few of the key examples will highlight to the modeller, the requirement for accurate research in order to create a DS model. Some colours (with AC codings) lasted just two or three seasons; others were used for years. The modeller must research the relevant body-to-roof colour or finish for these early DS years. British-, Belgian- and Australian-built DSs used sometimes unique paint and trim colours and fittings in comparison to French-built cars.

1956–61: Main colours: Noir (AC200), Vert Printemps (505), Aubergine (AC406), Champagne (AC134), Gris Rose (AC136), Jonquille (AC305), Bleu Nuage (AC604), Bleu Delphinium (AC603), Ecaille Blonde (AC306), Marron Glace (AC143), Jaune Panam (AC307), Vert Meleze (AC507), Rouge Esteral (AC408), Bleu Monte Carlo (AC605), Gris Mouette (AC146), Gris Typhon (AC147), Ambre Dore (AC308), Bleu Pacifique (AC607).

Later popular DS colours offered between 1962–75 at various model years, included: Gris Sable (AC104), Rouge Carmin (AC411), Bleu d'Orient (AC616), Gris Palladium (AC108), Rouge Cournaline (ACAC419), Gris Kandahar (AC133), Bordeaux (AC421), Vert Chamille (AC522), Bleu Platine (AC632), Sable (AC318), BlacnAlbatros (AC087), Rouge Massena (AC423), Beige Thonolet (AC085), Brun Carabee (AC427), Bleu Delta (AC640).

Inside the DS, a vast array of materials, synthetics, leather, plastics, chromium plate and nylon mouldings covered everything from the dashboard to the doors to the seats. For the modeller, rendering Citroën's Rhovyline, Jersey, Hellanca, Similoid, Targa, Cantrail cloths, fabrics and plastic finishes or the special effect leathers, requires much modelling skill.

Ebbro of Japan created their DS 19 and DS 21 1/24-scale kits with high-quality parts and excellent, accurate rendition of key components. This is the box art for their DS 19 – which could, of course, be adapted to any DS year specification by the expert modeller.

Fabrice Maréchal: Model Maker Extraordinaire

Top professional model maker Fabrice Maréchal (see Fabrice Maréchal Models online) is well known in the modelling community for his stunning, high-quality model-building standards that have also featured in magazines and online modeller sites. A Belgium-based professional modeller, Patrice has been commissioned by collectors and manufacturers to create his sublime in-depth three-dimensional models that really do look like the real thing – especially in terms of paint and trim finish. His Formula One and racing car models are greatly respected in the community.

Patrice provides build stories and tutorials of his builds via the Modelersite.com enthusiast website and one look at his works will convince you of his quality standards. For over a decade Patrice's models have gained a reputation for accuracy and stunning paintwork that is carefully built up to produce 'in the metal' appearance. See his works at Modelersite.com and at Scalecar.net and a range of online portals and in-print publications.

Patrice worked on the Ebbro Citroën DS 19 1/24-scale release at an early stage (via the manufacturer) and tackled many of the issues inherent in creating an accurate rendition of the DS and its specific type variant. He did, however, favour some small level of artistic licence in the paint hues, seemingly to complement the DS, not detract from it.

Fabrice here provides his own commentary for readers to follow for their build of the DS 19 kit – note also the DS 21 kit details:

Ebbro (#25005) DS 19, 1/24. Also available as the Ebbro/Tamiya (#25009) DS 21, 1/24 depicting the post-1967 car.

DS 19 Details with Fabrice Maréchal

Ebbro provided an opportunity to make the most of their injection mould of the DS 19 but as I looked at

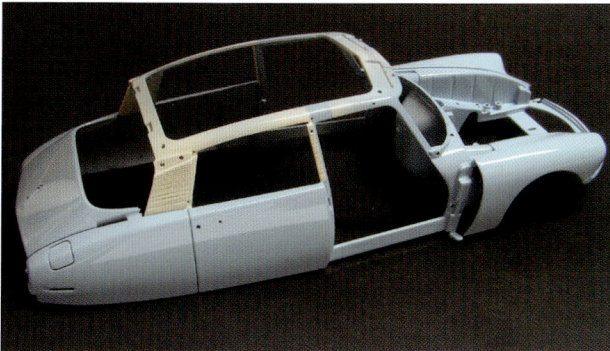

As described in the accompanying text, Fabrice built up the car chassis caisson and the bodywork in a manner not dissimilar to the real DS.

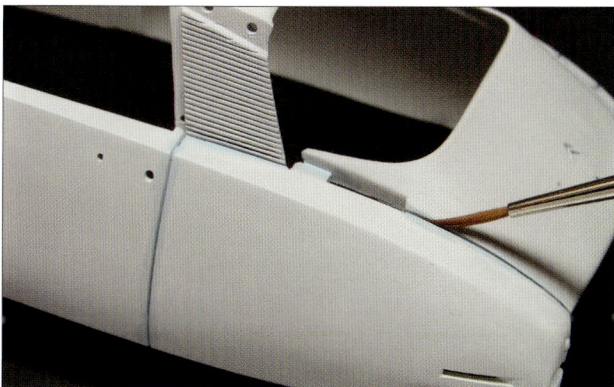

this build, it was obvious that I had to make sure about certain points of the car's details.

I looked for original pictures that could help me but it was important to realize that many of the pictures I found were of restored cars – which do not guarantee the accuracy of the original production-car specification, yet many of the old pictures are not of the highest quality for noting specific details.

Because this build was a pre-production model, there were minimal instructions available, so there was research to do. I think the final result is a model that represents the spirit of the DS.

To comment on the rear roof pillars: the C-pillars came in many differing finishes on the production-car DS and Ebbro have represented this detail very well (in their specific model's moulding) to match the real thing and in the correct manner for this type of DS 19 rear C-pillar. I decided to slightly accentuate the lines to capture the scale depth effect and did so by scribing them to a very slightly enhanced depth.

Fresh out of the dies, an obvious point was that the front windscreen surround was a vital aspect of the DS build but needed a touch more definition at this pre-production stage.

The under-chassis (or caisson) was built up, the cabin built in, and the external body panels attached. I built the car with the adjustable suspension in a higher setting position, with rear wheels glued to suspension arms. Once constructed, the passenger compartment was glued to the chassis base unit. Epoxy glue was placed on the mounting points of the chassis for the body attachment.

I made small modifications to windscreen A-pillars to improve the fit of the vital exterior trims. The windscreen was placed into its frame then fixed with cyanoacrylate d4 with one drop top and bottom but of course being very careful not to let glue affect the plastic 'glass' moulding (cyano being a risk). I used white Tron glue by capillary action to the secure the contours of the windscreen. The rear window was fitted by being interlocked into the mouldings then glued. The side windows were firmly fixed in to avoid problems fitting the cabin interior door trims.

The dashboard moulding is in my view the lower point of the kit as the moulding is lacking in fine detail. I worked on it with care and paint but texture was difficult to achieve. Then I fitted the dashboard

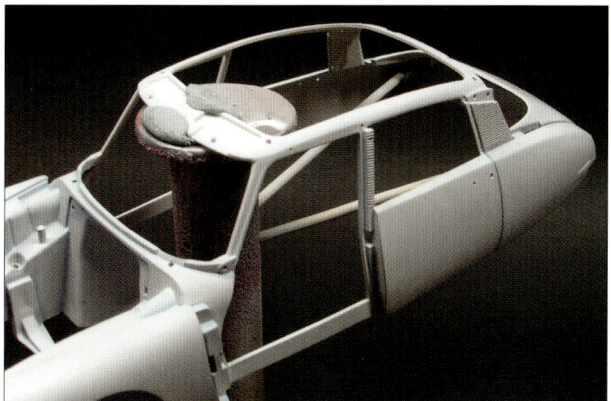

This view shows us what careful and forensic preparation can create during a kit build. Of note, the Ebbro kit resembles the real car's construction and build process.

Here we see careful attention being applied to the shut lines and panel gaps in order to create the best possible outcome (see text for types of materials used).

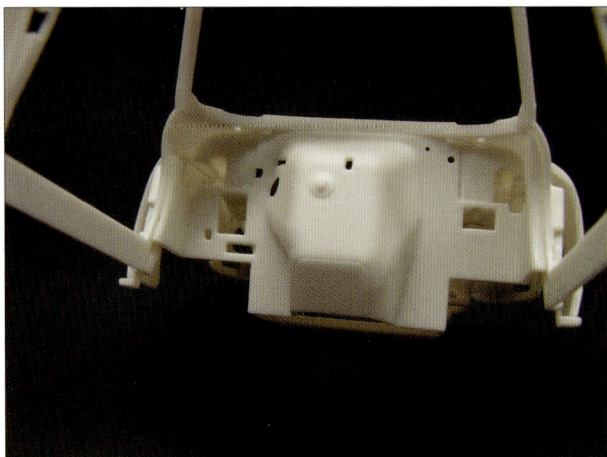

A rare view from inside the body of the front bulkheads during the construction process and showing off Ebbro's uncanny accuracy in relation to the 'real' thing.

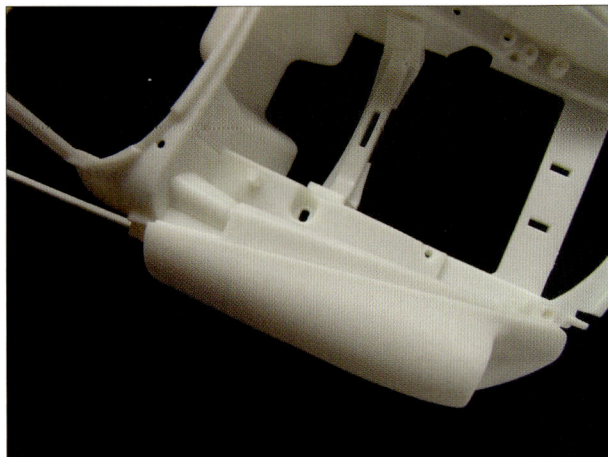

The front wings and scuttle prior to paintings. All cross-members and panels are to scale.

Masked up and with the caisson and body parts joined, ready for the interior. Having re-detailed the C-pillar ribs, Fabrice then gently primed prior to painting and ensured that no detail depth was lost due to primer; he avoided over-thickness.

A key aspect of any DS build is the windscreen-to-roof intersection and the vital trim panels that surround it. This is where expert-level care is required in the build (see text). The engine bearers and sub-chassi s are ready to accept the mechanicals.

and steering column. The front seats and back seat were finished in Desert Yellow XF60 (a good match to the original trim material colour).

Prior to painting, the body shell was washed, then grey-primered with a brush to all engraved cast details: but be careful not to fill in the depth of the mouldings – so as not to lose detail. My advice (as with full-size body finishing) is to build thin layers of primer, but *not* to be used to cover up flaws. This can be done with Tamiya white spray primer.

I use Gravity Colors paint and having masked up, I used artistic licence with the Gulf Blue paint code basis which, although not a true Citroën colour, is a very close match to Citroën Bleu Nuage that I felt complemented the model (readers should note that Bleu Nuage, or cloud blue, was not deployed on the production DS until the 1959 model year).

After the thin layers of primer, I sanded with 1500 then cleaned. I built up several very thin layers of paint (which is preferable to having too much paint at an early stage). The roof was painted ivory to match the DS 19 roof colour options. The Gravity Colors built up very well with even covering. I then (very lightly) sanded with 4000 micromesh water-based abrasive to as to give a good key to the varnish/lacquer-finish layer.

Prior to final paint-sealing varnish, a gentle blank assembly of all bodywork, the caisson and cabin was

carried out. The front bumper was the last to go on and headlamp detailing required a special technique. Interesting details include the headlamps, which I fitted by removing centring pins so that they could be glued without having to touch up the chrome ring trim afterwards – giving a much cleaner finish. Of note, indicator lens colours of the DS year-1956 car were a different colour, being white not orange.

The doors were easily attached to the body via their hinges and I used black paint to show the rubber door seals – specifically for the open door that I decided to use on this model build.

After building up the chassis, I then moved onto the engine bay. Engine and main bulkhead were installed directly (the dashboard installed later). After construction, I airbrushed the engine bay (and also the rear underside of the body) in TS29 satin black. The engine bay was dry-brushed matte black 33 and flesh colour Humbrol 61.

The engine was in two parts and engine, oil sump and gearbox all need to be built and finished separately. I airbrushed in X5 green the parts that DS was specified with on the production car.

The gearbox and the engine's cylinder head were finished in XF16 aluminium and the oil sump in XF56 steel. I used Tamiya dark brown – to texturize and treat relevant surfaces. I then used metalizer steel

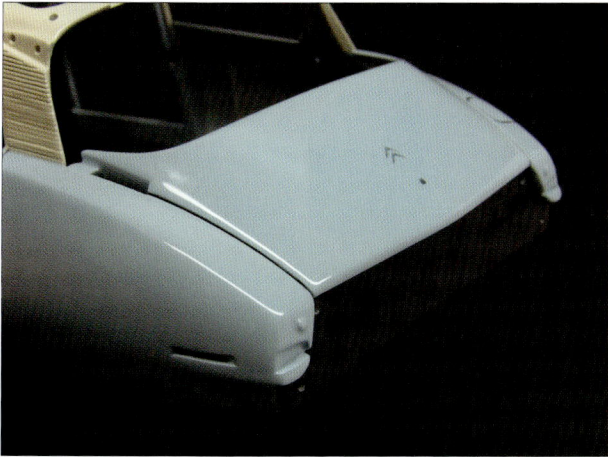

Fabrice carried out much preparation and finessing to the body, notably at the rear and to the chevron engraving in the boot/trunk lid moulding.

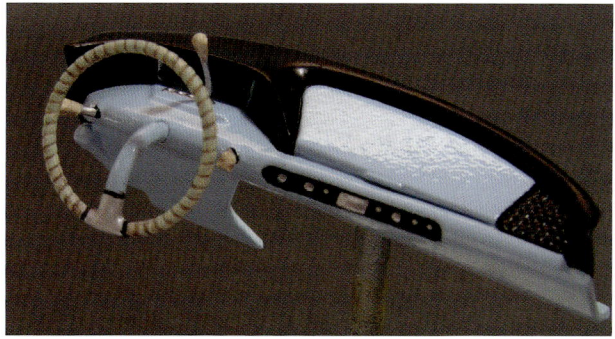

As you can see, hard work paid off. Note the correct (wider) weave to the late-1956 steering wheel tape.

Above: The DS had a flat floor. Here you can also see the wheel/axle stubs and the suspension's hydraulic spheres.
Left: Superb detailing and painting using various paints (see text) produced this wonderful rendition of the DS engine.

colour on components such as the brake discs. I treated the exhaust manifold in burnt metal. Patina was correctly achieved.

Of note, I had a small problem with the under-bonnet/hood spare tyre and its wheel rim in this early moulding; both items had to be thinned down in gauge to ensure clearance with bonnet/hood closure.

Both driveshafts were fitted after the engine was mounted into the body, then the front wheels attached, noting some work being needed on the attachment to axle/lug details.

Wipers, door handles, mirrors and the middle B-pillar lights were all vital details to be correctly added. Such details are critical to the quality achieved. As an example, I enhanced the boot/trunk lid chevron badge to make it stand out as a detail, not just as a chrome piece. Silver paint was put onto the engraving to make it stand out.

An interesting detail was the boot/trunk lid release button – as it is seemingly from the 1959 production-car model year onwards and not Ebbro's 1956-suggested specification. A button without a latch piece was more correct, as modified.

I also removed some slight excess in the moulding ribs on the wings. Overall, however, the moulding has finesse and the correct radius and curvatures to the panels – notably the shape of the roof.

In sum, as can be seen in the accompanying photographs, Ebbro have delivered a very beautiful kit, where the precision of the assemblies/mouldings is flawless. I am sure that the model maker, tempted by the assembly of this DS, will find that the kit and

my build tutorial will provide the techniques to build the DS of their dreams.

Paints and materials used:

Spray paint, Tamiya: TS-13, TS-29.
Acrylic, Tamiya: X-5, X-26, X-27, XF-2, XF-16, XF-55, XF-56, XF-60, XF-63, XF-69.
Panel Line Accent Colour, Tamiya: Dark Brown.
Enamels, Humbrol: 11, 33, 60, 61, 62. Model Master: Metal (1415), Steel (1402), Aluminium (1401).
Oil paint, Windsor & Newton: Natural Earth, Black.
Gravity Colors: primer GC-303, Ivory GC-121, Gulf Blue GC-108, Gloss Clear Box Set.
Products used in the build: Colle cyanoacrylate, Epoxy, Tron SP104, Revell turpentine rectifier. Abrasives: Gelson polish, Tamiya modelling wax.

For the die-cast enthusiast and the resin/plastic-injection-moulded kit builder, the sheer range of DS offerings and specifications can either be seen as a challenge or, more likely, a collectors' opportunity to indulge in the celebration and creation of a spectacular car design that is unlikely ever to be repeated. Here lies history, design language, an industrial design legacy and a superb car amid a tangible modelling legacy in one of the best stories of not just French car design, but global automotive success and intelligence in the mid-twentieth century. André Citroën would surely have approved. Yet how odd it is that DS is now a branding and marketing machine that has little to do with the actual DS, the *real* DS.

Acknowledgements
The author wishes to thank the following people and respective sources in the creation of this book: Julian Marsh/Citroënet. org.uk; Citroënvie; David Conway; Darrin Brownhill at Citroën Classics (Staines); Citroën SM Club GB & Brian Long; the late David Evans; Citroën Car Club UK; Citroën Press Office UK; Conservatoire Citroën and Citroën Press office photo archives; PSA.S.A. Norev; John Ayrey Die-Casts; *Practical Classics*; *Classic Cars*; Jon Pressnell's *Citroën DS: The Complete Story*, published by the Crowood Press; *Citroën: The Complete Story* by Lance Cole, published by the Crowood Press; *Original Citroën DS* by John Reynolds with Jan de Lange, published by Bay View Books; Russell Wallis/RJWDesign; Fabrice Maréchal (Fabrice Maréchal Models); Modelersite. com; and Prescott Hill Climb/Bugatti Owners' Club La Vie en Bleu. Thanks lastly to my late grandfather Thomas Robert Godden – Citroën DS owner and pilot. Please note that the author Lance F. Cole has no connection with Lance Cole Photography, its website or actions.